THE URBAN HEN

Visit our How To website at www.howto.co.uk

At www.howto.co.uk you can engage in conversation with our authors – all of whom have 'been there and done that' in their specialist fields. You can get access to special offers and additional content but most importantly you will be able to engage with, and become a part of, a wide and growing community of people just like yourself.

At www.howto.co.uk you'll be able to talk and share tips with people who have similar interests and are facing similar challenges in their lives. People who, just like you, have the desire to change their lives for the better – be it through moving to a new country, starting a new business, growing their own vegetables, or writing a novel.

At www.howto.co.uk you'll find the support and encouragement you need to help make your aspirations a reality.

You can also go directly to www.the-urban-hen.co.uk which is part of the main How To website.

How To Books strives to present authentic, inspiring, practical information in their books. Now, when you buy a title from **How To Books,** you get even more than just words on a page.

THE URBAN HEN

A practical
guide to
keeping poultry
in a town or city

Paul Peacock

SPRING HILL

Published by Spring Hill

Spring Hill is an imprint of How To Books Ltd
Spring Hill House, Spring Hill Road,
Begbroke, Oxford, OX5 1RX, United Kingdom
Tel: (01865) 375794 Fax: (01865) 379162
info@howtobooks.co.uk
www.howtobooks.co.uk

How To Books greatly reduce the carbon footprint of their books by sourcing their typesetting
and printing in the UK.

First edition 2009

British Library Cataloguing in Publication Data
A catalogue record for this book is available from the British Library

ISBN: 978 1 905862 27 6

Text illustrations by Rebecca Peacock
Produced for How To Books by Deer Park Productions, Tavistock
Typeset by TW Typesetting, Plymouth, Devon
Printed and bound by Bell & Bain Ltd, Glasgow

CONTENTS

INTRODUCTION

Read this, it's probably the best part of the book.

The best place for a chicken is to be with a human that will understand and care for it properly. Keeping hens in the town is possibly the first step to human independence at the family level, but it does need some working at, and consequently this book explores some of the aspects of keeping poultry in confined spaces.

FREE RANGE OR NOT?

Free-range chickens are allowed to roam, within reason, almost wherever they want to. That's the general perception anyway. Commercial free-range birds might only ever have as much space as a sheet of A4 to themselves, but they can move around. Organic free-range hens have fields and feed and freedom, but you can give them an even better experience of life in your own garden.

A modern hen hut, be it made from wood as in an ark or plastic as in the eglu, comes with a run either at the side of the hut or underneath it. This way the birds can come outside and enjoy plenty of fresh air in a protected zone from predators.

This isn't exactly free range, but is perfect for a couple of birds. All they need is food, water, a little free space and a partner! Perfect!

POLLUTION

Some urban spaces have problems from their history. My first hens were kept in a garden that I found out later to be contaminated with some dreadful chemicals from a local factory and I had to replace the soil. Thankfully the Clean Air Act has made atmospheric pollution much better, but I would hesitate keeping hens within a few metres of a major road, partly for the noise and disturbance to the birds and partly because of the benzene derivatives that come in exhaust.

Be careful about where you site the birds and take careful note of sewage, soil-borne pollution, noise, smoke and air pollution, oil and general rubbish. Try to keep them in quiet, clean places that are safe from predators. If you happen to live near a municipal tip or waste disposal centre then protect your birds from gulls and take extra precautions against rats.

REGIME

I have outlined a regime that most poultry keepers would find onerous simply to emphasise the extra care needed in an urban situation. Poultry keeping in the town, where the neighbours abut on either side of the garden fence has implications not found in the less urban situation. Above all, this means removing food at night and keeping stores of food away from rats and mice.

These two animals are the cause of more complaints than anything else, and you should make sure your hens are kept in pristine conditions, not for their sake, but for the neighbours!

WHY KEEP HENS AT ALL?

The supermarket shelves are full of eggs; the cold displays are full of chicken meat. You can buy free-range chicken meat and eggs from ultra cosseted hens on farms that would be considered a five star hen hotel, if you like. You can also buy the other sort for a lot less money. Buy why keep hens at all when it makes financial sense to simply buy their products from the supermarkets? You can certainly buy according to your conscience, and still make a good saving compared to keeping the birds themselves.

The simple answer is that hens are lovely; poultry are pretty and simply being near them gladdens the heart and lifts the spirit. Hens are a wonderful contradiction between vulnerability and ruggedness. They are capable of living happily in the most extreme circumstances and yet one is left with the overwhelming desire to care for them.

They are the very best way of instigating a sense of care and responsibility in children, individual tasks are not usually onerous or difficult to understand. Their simple needs are easy to grasp and when a child assimilates the needs of another creature and does something to meet those needs, civilisation is in good hands.

There are material benefits – great eggs for one. Maybe you have never tasted a fried egg that was laid minutes ago. It is a wholly different experience; the yolk sits proud of a firm white and the egg doesn't swill around the pan as though it was mostly water, which it is. Fresh eggs are a boon, whichever hen they come from. The eggs of a Rhode Island Red are big, round and rich, but contain no more nutrients than the smaller egg of a bantam.

Secondary benefits include a never-ending supply of manure for the garden. Hens produce about a handful of manure a day; over a year that's a lot of handfuls! Manure produced by poultry is excellent for composting, perfect for cabbages and other brassicas, and is the mushroom growing medium par excellence. Mixed with straw you can get a year round supply of breakfast mushrooms to go with your breakfast eggs. If only chickens laid bacon.

WHY KEEP HENS IN TOWN?

Why do people complain about hens in the garden? A list of the complaints I have had on an inner city estate in Manchester:

They attract rats

They smell

They are unhygienic

They spread diseases

It's cruel

They are noisy

Their housing is ugly

They fly over the fence and spoil my garden

They will attack the children

They frighten my poodle

Hens don't attract rats

Rats are not interested in poultry at all. They are interested in the excess food left behind when we feed poultry too much. There are two measures you need to ensure hens are not attracting rats. They need a house to sleep in and lay that stands proud of the earth. If there is daylight between the floor and the hen hut, you are most likely not to ever see a rat. Secondly, only feed the hens enough for the day and remove the excess at night. Then keep the feed away from the hens, in some locked cupboard, and you are more or less guaranteed to never see a rat.

Hens don't smell

Well they do, a bit. It's a pleasant smell. They smell bad when they are not cleaned out; they are fed food from the kitchen that is not eaten and goes off when left. They smell when the litter is not cleaned away and droppings left to build up for weeks on end.

In truth, hens are very easy on the nose if looked after properly. It should be mentioned that you do need to work harder at keeping birds in the city than in the country simply because there are not so many people in the country to notice smells or complain about this or that.

Hens are not unhygienic

On the contrary, they spend hours cleaning themselves. Hygiene problems occur when the hen is not carefully cared for. Very little care is needed to keep both hens and the neighbours happy. There is no real reason why they should be noticed at all.

Hens do not spread diseases

By now you are getting the point that hens are perfectly safe. Recent problems with salmonella have largely been eradicated by stringent inoculation, and you are probably never going to buy a hen that has not already been treated for the disease. Poultry diseases do not affect people on the whole and as long as a basic regime of feeding and cleaning is maintained there should be no problems at all.

Avian flu is nothing to do with chickens per se, being brought into the country by wild birds, usually geese and swans. The chances of a wild animal causing your flock any problems are as near to zero as to make no difference. A passing bird is just as likely to let its droppings fall on your neighbour.

It is not cruel to keep hens in town

Anyone keeping chickens in a responsible, informed manner are doing hen-kind a great service. One more in a back garden with room to roam, one less in a battery cage or, worse still, a huge chicken shed living an Orwellian nightmare.

Hens are not noisy

Cockerels are – but you don't need them. Hens make soft, warm chuckles in the morning, quite conducive to sleep. When they are laying they make louder chuckles, and maybe the odd screech (well you try doing it!), but that's all. By the time the neighbours have heard the chuckling, the bok bocking, they will smile in amusement at the egg laying noises. Another one from Gerty!

Hen houses don't have to be ugly

You could knock a few boxes together and shelter hens in them and it would make a very comfortable home. But you can make with a little care or buy cheaply some very presentable structures for keeping hens. There are some hen houses that will make the neighbours positively green with envy. There are huts out there made from plastic and wood, and the designs are never ending. A well thought out hen house will add value to the garden and consequently the house.

Hens don't have to fly

I bought hens at a market for the first time, knowing nothing about them. I put them into my hen run on the allotment and the next morning they were all over the plots eating other people's vegetables. I learned the lesson pretty quick that if you trim the flight feathers on one wing the birds cannot get over the fence in the first place. This process doesn't hurt the hens – it's just like going for a haircut.

They don't have to attack the children

A cockerel might, if allowed, attack any small child. It's their way. Females never attack anyone unless provoked. The answer is not to keep cockerels. You don't need them for eggs and unless you like their fine colours, or want to breed from them or you are going to eat them, they are a waste of food in the urban garden.

They frighten my poodle

Don't buy a poodle. Self evident that one. Truthfully, introducing pets together is a controlled affair. You can condition your pets to encounters with hens very easily and within a short time you can have them coexisting comfortably.

CHECK YOUR DEEDS – ARE YOU ALLOWED TO KEEP POULTRY?

Before you embark on keeping hens in the garden you need to have a check on the deeds to your property. If you live in a house that is pre WW2 then you should have no problems about keeping livestock unless you live in very select London suburbs like Kensington, where the control of livestock by deed was more common pre war.

The only legal objection to keeping poultry will be found in the deeds to your house. If there is no embargo on livestock, you can go ahead.

If you live in a council house there is a longstanding right for people to be able to keep poultry in gardens. There have been a number of attempts to do away with this but the recent upsurge in poultry keeping has meant that for the most part council properties still allow poultry so long as there is a garden big enough to accommodate them. If there is an objection to keeping poultry on council property it will be listed in your tenancy agreement.

The situation with private tenants is somewhat different. Each landlord can decide for him or herself if they are going to permit poultry on the property, even if the original deeds to the house raise no objections. Again, check your tenancy agreement.

YOU HAVE TO WORK HARDER TO KEEP HENS IN THE CITY

In all cases, whether you own your own property or you rent it, you have to be extra vigilant. If your neighbour or landlord objects to you keeping hens in the garden there are many ways they can stop you. They can complain to the health inspector, the environmental health department, the rent office and so on. They can claim nuisance and get you into all sorts of trouble with the RSPCA just by complaining.

You need to demonstrate at all times that you are taking utmost care with the animal's welfare, the cleanliness of the garden, the way you remove and compost the litter, everything. And on top of this, a box of eggs every now and then goes a long way to keeping everyone happy.

You need to keep everyone happy if you are going to keep hens in an urban garden!

A WORD ABOUT HOLIDAYS

Poultry should never be left alone to fend for themselves. The bonus about hens is that they don't miss you, and they are therefore easy animals to foster out to another poultry lover. If you are going to ask a neighbour to look after them, make sure they have been through the routine several times before letting them loose on your girls. You don't want a bill from the fire brigade for rescuing your animals from the top of the church roof.

CHAPTER 1
NEW TO CHICKENS

The decision to keep chickens in the garden at home is an exciting one, but now there is much to be done and things to consider. This chapter will tell you how to prepare for your first hens, where to house them and what to house them in.

HENS IN THE GARDEN

Security

Security in the garden is paramount. You should have a good set of fencing that people cannot get over or through and if possible the same goes for other people's pets. Lay garden shale or stones on the floor so you can hear unwanted visitors approach the house and if you have room an impenetrable and painful looking hedge inside the fences will act as a double deterrent. My own garden is only 10 metres long by 10 metres wide, but by the path at the

end I have 2.5 metres of thick hedge that not even an elephant could push through.

More than anything you should put your hen hut out of sight. The less attention you draw to them the better. This will cut down worries from the neighbours and unwanted attention from youths. Most young people are wonderful, inquisitive and love to admire chickens. The idea of hens providing eggs is fascinating to young people and, having shown them, you will usually find they are not only protective and loyal but they respect the idea that hens need peace.

However, there are too many instances of vandalism and it is wise to keep your birds in a protected position.

Physical factors

Hens do well in bright, airy, calm conditions. They love a little shade in the summer and protection from driving rain in the winter. They like to scratch in the ground and eat insects and worms and they prefer to wander and perch. They love to explore and hunt out insects from around the garden.

Perhaps the best thing is to place the hen house behind a single screen for privacy in a place where they are not overlooked. A tree or bush will provide some shelter from sunlight.

What happens to the grass

Hens scratch in the soil – they love it! There is nothing more encouraging to see their demeanour change when they are scratching and eating insects and worms. They also poo on the grass. If you have too many hens the grass soon becomes a muddy mess.

On the other hand, the hens do build up an excess of parasites if they are on the same ground all the time. To prevent this they should either be allowed to roam over a wide area, so you need a big garden, or they should be restricted to a pit where you can remove the soil and the parasites altogether.

You can make or buy a hut with a run suitable for a few hens (often enough) and the run area can be dug out and lined with pond liner. On top of this you can put any number of substrates: woodchip, compost and woodchip mixed, soil, even roll out some turf. Then after a few weeks this can be removed and composted.

PREDATORS

Raptors

Everyone knows Mr Fox, but fewer know the impact of the increased population of raptors (birds of prey) in the city. In particular the increasing numbers of sparrowhawks in the city has become a particular threat. They will have a go at bantams, which they relish, but a full-sized hen is more of a challenge. However it is a challenge they are increasingly taking up. Trees make their task harder, and a run with a mesh roof is also important.

Foxes

The fox in the city is a sad beast. Anyone knowing the proud animal that leanly fleets around the countryside is saddened at their scavenging around the town, tipping dustbins and, in a fit of wildness, attacking chickens in gardens. He is best kept at bay with good security at the perimeter of the garden. Once they locate hens they will return time and again. Keep an eye out for signs of intrusion and, if you see any, be on the look out to scare the fox away. Once challenged they are much more skittish and will eventually give up if challenged nightly.

We will look at this in more detail, but the hen house should not present any loose parts that give encouragement to a hard working paw. Make sure that the run is protected by good stiff mesh capable of taking punishment from a medium-sized wild animal, that the mesh is buried a foot under the ground and that any joins in the mesh are not only overlapped, but securely wired together.

Rats

These animals tend not to attack the hens themselves, but are more interested in the excess food. They are adept, however, at killing chicks and breaking into eggs. They are highly intelligent creatures and on their guard as to approaching humans.

At some time or other rats will appear in the garden – after all the people on our street leave much more food about than the chickens do, and there are lots of rats about the place, it's just that we are not used to seeing them.

The problem with rats is not the animals themselves, but the diseases they carry. Everyone associates bubonic plague with rats but thankfully this no longer is a threat in the UK, though some people have recently contracted it in the United States.

WEIL'S DISEASE

This is also known as leptospirosis and is contracted via a bacterium, Leptospira interrogans. This causes a wide-ranging set of symptoms and can be controlled by antibiotics. It sometimes results in hospitalisation and in very rare cases will kill. About one in five rats carry the bacterium and they spread it around in their urine. Swimmers sometimes contract the disease and more commonly fishermen, who get it from water contaminated with rat urine.

When you are cleaning your hut or around the chickens, always wear protective gloves and clothing. You are only in danger of becoming ill if infected liquid gets into the blood, so be sure you do not work with open cuts.

If you see or suspect rats being in the area you should do something about it straight away. You can lay traps for them, poison them and keep a good ratter (dog or cat), but the numbers of rats are probably quite large, them coming from the general area. It is a good idea to raise the hen hut off the ground so that they cannot settle beneath and disguise the area by growing onions and garlic all around.

The main defence against rats is to make sure the area is constantly and scrupulously clean, with no food left around for them to steal and continued vigilance.

HEN HOUSING

Simply because we are used to seeing hens kept in the most cramped conditions doesn't mean this should be replicated in the garden. Hen houses should allow all the birds that use it to flap their wings (both at the same time) and have a decent volume of fresh air. There are certain small pyramidal type houses, normally referred to as arcs, which would really be suitable for only a single bird. They tend only to parade down the centre of the unit where there is greatest height.

If you are going to buy such a design it is best that you get the largest you can afford. Alternatively only keep one or two birds in a small arc. The runs associated with this type of house are also quite small.

Pecking order and small huts

If you keep two (or more) birds in a confined space they will do what comes naturally and sort out who is boss and who is not. In a confined space this becomes a problem because simple clucking and pecking turns into bullying. Pecking syndrome, which we shall look at later, often leads to the death of the victim and the birds that are doing the pecking are difficult to get out of the habit. This syndrome is exacerbated by a lack of room.

If you are buying a wooden hut make sure it is made from 19 mm ply at least. Such a lot of wood is hard to move around the garden for sure, but is enough protection for the birds against weather and predators, so long as the door is strong and tightly fitting. This thickness of wood provides thermal insulation for both hot days and cold nights. Make sure there is also adequate insulation.

Panting and small huts

Chickens, like dogs, sweat into their breath. A considerable amount of water is evaporated in exhaled breath and this tends to collect in the bedding material. Too many birds in small huts get colds very easily, something shown by comparing birds that roost in huts and birds that roost in trees. The tree roosted birds hardly ever get colds, but too many birds in a small hut frequently are unwell.

Just to reiterate, a small hut is not necessarily a bad thing, so long as you do not cram too many birds into it.

Plastic huts

For some reason traditional poultry keepers have looked askance at plastic huts, yet more than 20,000 people have bought one model in only a few years. There are two basic designs, a small one which is suitable for a couple of birds only, and a large one which holds around ten. There have been various outcries against these units with very little justification.

In particular, apart from being an asset in the garden, they do look good, no other unit is as well insulated and they will never need to be repaired. They provide the perfect barrier to predators because there is nothing to fall off or get scratched away.

The big thing about plastic is that it presents no little niches for parasites to build up. One of the less pleasant aspects of dealing with hens is they get mites easily. The worst of these is red mite that hides in wooden perches during the day and climbs onto the chicken's legs at night to drink avian blood. The big problem is that wood provides hiding spaces in the blemishes and cracks, and around the edge and so on. But a plastic moulding provides no hiding place and the parasites are easily wiped away.

The old shed

Sheds are a great size for chickens to make their home. They are also easily cleaned because there is a lot of room. Make sure the structure is sufficient to keep draughts and foxes away, and the wood is firmly in place all around. Modern sheds are not made from good materials and will need reinforcing. As an example of this, if you live near badgers, they have been known to crash right through the walls of a shed to get at eggs and whatever else inside.

The interior of the hut

Traditionally poultry roost at night time and they take themselves to bed. When dusk arrives they will start to congregate around the hut, walk in, walk out, bok bok a lot and eventually they will get themselves inside and jump onto their perch. Their nights are spent more or less asleep, pooing and huddled reasonably close for warmth on cold nights.

The perch should be big enough for the hen to grip, around 2–3 in (5–8 cm), and you should provide a low one at around 18 in (45 cm) and another twice this height.

However, some designs of hut have bars for perching at a low level, and you need to consider this when you buy. Space saving isn't always the best for the birds and I do believe they prefer to be higher off the ground than some huts provide for. I say this because in the wild Indian poultry roost in trees, so it must be a natural thing to get up high.

The floor needs to be absorbent because the chickens will poo when on the perch, sometimes against the wall too. If you can get a ready supply of sawdust, particularly pine sawdust, this makes an excellent material for the floor. The oils in the pine dust give the hut a pleasant aroma. Other materials include bark and wood chippings as well as straw, which I like because it adds insulation.

In an urban situation I would suggest you change your bedding at least once a month. It is compostable, but you might find you have more material than space. If you use straw as bedding it is perfect for growing mushrooms.

The nest box

In some place in the hut you should create a nesting area. These should be like hen-sized cubicles with an inviting dish of straw in them. The birds will squat in the space and lay. More often than not the hen will vacate the box and another will climb in to lay herself. The sight of the egg in the box is enough to encourage the other birds to follow suit. Some designs allow you to collect the eggs from outside the hut via a trap door.

The nesting boxes should be away from the roosting area, and if possible the entrance to the house should not go past the nesting area either, though this last point is not so important. Try to make sure that no food gets into the nesting area. The old time poultry keepers used to use orange boxes for nesting because they seemed to be exactly the right size. They should be, if possible, at the darkest part of the shed.

It is a good idea to collect eggs every day and change the straw lining every few days so that parasites don't build up inside.

A word about bedding

The material you lay in the hut for the comfort of the birds has a multi-functional role. First it is something warm and comfy for the hen to sit on, especially when laying. Hay is probably the most convenient material for this, though in an emergency I have used ripped newspaper. The material laid on the floor might provide some insulation, but its major function is absorbance of dropped poo by the hens while on the perch. I also like to have something that will dry the feet when they walk inside. There are a number of possibilities for this and usually I rely on sheets of newspaper and sawdust. I have a supply of strong smelling pine sawdust which not only disguises the aroma of the birds (helping with predators and rats) but gives me the illusion at least that the hut is clean and disinfected. Since I clean the hut every week anyway, the newspaper seems to last that long.

Alternatively you can use hay to cover the floor or, if you have wood chippings outside, you can continue this inside too. People who keep horses have a lot of bedding solutions from pelleted paper to straw. These can be used as bedding so long as they are not too crumbly and interesting enough to tempt the birds to eat it.

Food in the house

There are some, mostly homemade, huts that have a storage area for food and hooks from the roof on which feeders can hang. As a general rule, do not feed your hens inside the hut and store the feed in some other place altogether, where rats and mice cannot get to it.

No matter how careful you are regarding food, some will be spilt and this is the major cause for rats in the garden. It will not take long for you to determine exactly how much food your birds are consuming and feed this in a tray, or small hopper outside. Make it a part of your daily regime to clean all the feed away.

Light

The egg laying/moulting cycle is determined by the length of the day and, if your hut is in a dark position, perhaps made with wood and is quite light tight, the birds will come in to lay a couple of weeks later than if they had a good window. Similarly, ventilation is an important part of the house. A small, wire mesh window is a good idea wherever it is practicable. Pre-constructed huts should have adequate ventilation.

The run

If your garden is secure enough then you might wish to leave your birds roaming it freely. In this case a couple of hens in a small garden should have enough space to wander, forage and poo with few problems. The absolute minimum for this should be around 8 m² per bird, but twice this would be better.

If you do not have enough security to allow the birds free range around the garden a mesh run is second best. This mesh should be very stout and secure, with an overlap which can be either buried or weighted down along its length to stop predators getting in.

Dust

You should provide some dust for the birds to bathe in. A box buried into the soil with a combination of compost, perhaps some sieved ashes and sand is ideal for birds to come along and bathe in. This is their way of making sure the external parasites are kept at bay. If you can manage it, some way of keeping the dust box dry will extend its use.

Heating?

Over the years I have been asked the same question time and again. 'Should I heat my hen hutch in winter?' The emphatic answer is no. If the weather is such that the water is frozen in the waterer, the birds will need an extra feed to cope. A late afternoon feeding of milled corn usually makes the chickens hot while they digest it overnight.

Freezing

While we're on the subject we might as well look at freezing temperatures and what to do. Water is kept from freezing by adding a little glycerine. When there is a lot of snow on the ground the birds will probably venture out for a short while and then make for the warmth of the hut. Protect them from the wind, driving rain and mud. If the weather looks to be turning bad, cover the run and bring some large plants in pots near to the run for shelter.

A balanced diet, some green stuff and plenty of corn will see them through the worst of the weather and I always find they look healthier and stronger after bad weather.

CRITERIA FOR A HAPPY HEN

Criteria	Tick
Is the garden secure from people and predators?	
Are the hut and run secure from predators?	
Can you move the hut to fresh land or remove the material the hens are walking on?	
Is there sufficient shade and shelter?	
Is there sufficient sunlight?	
Can the hens scratch at the soil, bark, straw or compost?	
Can the birds move their wings in the hut?	
Can the birds reach their food easily without competition from others?	
Can you clean the hut easily?	
Can you keep the hut floor dry?	
Can you get at the eggs easily?	
Has the hut enough ventilation and light?	
Have you somewhere secure to keep food?	
Have you access to friendly and good advice?	

MINIMUM REQUIREMENTS

I hate talking about minimum requirements as though that's all you are going to accumulate. But you do need a good waterer and at least a good tray that is not easily kicked over by aggressive or hungry birds. The hen hut should be as we have described, and you do need some basic disinfectant to keep the hut in good hygienic order.

We have already mentioned the regime for feed, and if you use a hopper feeder – where the food falls into a tray so the birds can eat as much and as often as they like – place a large tray beneath to catch the drops so you can easily clear away.

Waterers are easy to use; you simply fill the bucket and place the base on the bottom and invert. Water should be changed at least every two days or so. Never let the inside of the bucket get covered with algae and always take special care to clean out the base because it gets somewhat mucky.

NOTES ON HOW TO BUY CHICKENS

Let us suppose you have bought your run and found a local supply of chicken feed. You are now ready to buy hens. There is a huge network of hen breeders and suppliers out there and you should shop around for the one that gives you the most help.

Valuing advice (or not as the case may be)

Like most hobbies keeping poultry is one where you are offered lots of advice. Some will be good and some not so good. So if you have chosen a certain path, don't be put off it by someone telling you it is wrong so long as the welfare of the birds is paramount. As long as you can fulfil the basic requirements for happy hens, take no notice. But good advice is always welcome, especially if you can find people whose situation is similar to yours.

What makes a good bird?

There is something that people are good at, recognising a sick animal. We get a feeling from the way the animal looks and moves around, about the brightness of the eyes and the shininess of the coat.

Point of lay (POL) hens should be animate, they should move around, have bright eyes and peck at food with interest. Avoid birds with discharge around the eyes, birds that are listless and have their eyes closed. Their legs should have a neutral or yellow colour and they should have no unsightly, rough or scaly growths of any kind. The wattles should be soft and clean, smooth and glossy and red in colour. The comb should be intact and without blotches. It might not be bright red but it should be uniform and clean.

Plumage should be tight against the body and not rough. It should have glossy and waxy feathers with no gaps or patches and there should be not many downy feathers. The vent should be slightly moist, clean and surrounded with soft feathers.

The beak should be intact, not 'debeaked', and the bird should not show any repetitive movements. Constantly shaking the head, attacking other poultry, being aggressive around food should all be avoided.

Birds purchased from reputable dealers should be vaccinated by 13 weeks. There is a long list of diseases the birds are vaccinated against and you can buy POL hens that have been raised according to the RSPCA Freedom Food Standards or the Lion Mark Standards, thus guaranteeing the flock have been raised with excellent animal welfare in mind.

Most dealers follow a vaccination regime similar to the one below, which comes from a company called Merrydale Poultry. However, all this does not guarantee a particular hen will be free from problems.

Chick vaccination programme

Age	Disease	Advised vaccine
Day 1	Mareks	Hatchery injection
Day 1 or 2	Salmonella	Lohmann TAD VacE*
Day 5–7	Coccidiosis	Paracox
Day 20	Infectious Bursal	Intervet Gumboro D78*
Day 28	Infectious Bursal – Gumboro	Intervet Gumboro D78*
Week 5	Classical Infectious Bronchitis/Newcastle Disease	Intervet MA5/CLONE*
Week 6	Salmonella Enteritidis	Lohmann TAD VacE*
Week 7	Variant Infectious Bronchitis	Intervet IB4/91*
Week 8	Avian Rhinotracheitis	Merial Nemovac*
Week 10	Classical Infectious Bronchitis/Newcastle Disease	Intervet MA5/CLONE 30*
Week 11	Variant Infectious Bronchitis	Fort Dodge IB Primer (D274)
Week 13	Avian Encephalomyelitis	Intervet Nobilis AE*
Weeks 15 or 16	Salmonella Enteritidis	Lohmann TAD VacE*
Before delivery	INAC/Newcastle/Infectious Bronchitis Egg Drop Syndrome 76	Intervet IBmulti + ND + ED (INAC)

*Vaccines administered via drinking water
Source: www.eden-livestock.co.uk

How many hens should I get?

It is a cruel thing to keep a singlet hen. Of course the number of hens you keep will be determined by how much space you have, but an urban space should not be overrun by poultry. Three birds as a minimum for an urban garden will provide a reasonable number of eggs and provide enough interest. Five or six hens are as much as an ordinary garden can cope with easily, and don't forget the neighbours!

INTRODUCING HENS TO THEIR NEW HOME

Let us suppose you have everything you need to keep hens carefully and easily. Bring your hens home in a carry box in a very well ventilated car or vehicle. Gone are the days when you can get poultry delivered through the post.

Hens are creatures of habit and if you put them in the run or just in the garden they might well decide to sleep in trees. The best thing to do is to put them in the hut with some food and water and leave them there for 24 hours, a whole day and night. This will then imprint on them that this is their home. Once they have spent a night in the hut they will stay there every night.

Once they have left the hut, confine them to the covered run for a few days so they can orientate themselves before allowing them to wander more freely.

How to hold hens

You need to get hold of your hen so you can check various things, its point of lay status or so that you can clip its wings, etc. The way to do this will vary from hen to hen. It is important that the birds are comfortable with you. Feed them regularly, get a rapport. If you can get them to eat near you or even out of your hand, a trust will be imprinted between you and your hens.

On occasion offer out your hand and stroke their backs, anything to confirm that human touch is not a threat. This should be your first job with all hens.

Catching the bird

Happy hens will normally come to you. Wait around for the bird to walk by you and you should be able to reach down and catch them with a complete grasp of the lower body. If you cannot get the body as a complete whole, go for the legs. Don't chase the bird all over the place, if you must, shoo it towards a corner, but keep it from panicking. If you fail to get the bird, bide your time because there will be plenty of other opportunities. The other birds will soon learn that having picked a hen from the ground its fate was peaceful and without threat. This will facilitate the easy and stress-free handling of the flock.

As soon as you have a grip of the bird – never the head or the wings, and never grasp for tail feathers – bring it close and move your grip underneath to grasp the legs, carefully but firmly. Never let the legs cross over, try to get a couple of fingers between them.

Try to point the bird with its rear away from you so if it poos you won't get messed.

Clipping wings

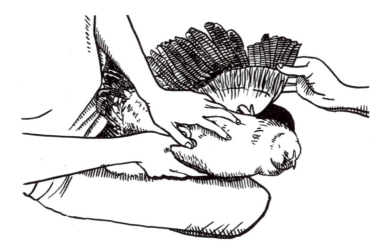

Hens can fly although they don't bother too much. A hen is capable of flying onto a roof quite easily and she can get over a fence with little effort. To prevent this, the flight feathers of one wing are trimmed a third of the way down their length from the tip.

If you trim both wings, a lighter bird will simply flap harder and get into the air. Trimming one side sends them into an unstable spin and they cannot control themselves enough to fly, so they don't bother. Eventually the feathers grow back, so you have to repeat the procedure. It isn't painful or cruel, it's a bit like a visit to the hairdressers – so long as you only clip a little of the wing.

Introducing new hens to established birds

Once you have bought and grown used to your hens it is almost guaranteed you will want to buy some more, maybe an attractive or unusual breed. New hens should not be simply plonked with established ones, even if there is room in the hut for them. Keep them separate for a week with an adjacent run so all the birds can see and get used to each other. Move their feed closer so they can eat together and assuming there are no flare-ups they can then be joined.

CHICKENS AND CHILDREN

There is not much difference between a child and a chicken. Both can be bossy, naughty, messy and noisy.

Chickens need not be a danger to your children. Apart from some cockerels, chickens are almost completely docile and safe, a complete joy for children to care for. In fact there is no better way of teaching children about caring, responsibility and the joys that the natural world brings.

Getting children to collect eggs and understand where they come from, and learning how fresh food is fantastic and good for you – there can be no better lessons in life; lessons difficult for schools to teach. So mixing kids and chickens at home is a must.

Get correct information

Don't stumble into buying chickens without thinking through all the facts. When some of the less pleasant aspects of keeping an animal occur, it can come as a shock to our plastic-coated pristine lives. That aside, chickens are perfect animals for the home.

Protecting the kids

It is probably best if you involve your children in the process of getting chickens right from the start. Get them to think about where the hens will go, what will it be like to keep them, what they will need, what kind of housing you should get and so on. Get them to work on all the questions that go through your own minds and find solutions to problems. Who will feed them? Who will collect the eggs? Who will clean them out? How will we keep them safe? All these are questions that should involve your children.

Avoiding the big peck off

If you have young children then shy away from cockerels who, let's face it, have nearly all the genetics of fighting game birds. But it isn't always possible to avoid cockerels, especially if you are hatching your own eggs (another marvellous thing for children to experience). But there are some things you can do to minimise potential problems.

Acclimatise your birds to the children by keeping them quiet and locked up, allowing the children to feed and water them, collect eggs and clean them out with supervision. Eventually the birds will become accustomed to them and coexist without problem.

What makes them flip?

Many years ago while at university I did some research into sign stimuli. We worked with hens and fighting fish and discovered that both the fish and the birds would attack certain shapes and colours but completely ignore others. So a cockerel would attack a red dot but not a white one. Now there are lots of different reasons why you should not take this as gospel, but sometimes a normally docile animal will attack for no obvious reason although it may transpire that the person was wearing clothes that excited the automatic response in the animal. As far as chickens go it is the comb colour that can excite, so avoid tops with red blobs on them. You have to remember that chickens don't look up so they first of all see at the level of a child's knee, so it's pants that are important.

Protecting the chickens

Children can be noisy and boisterous. A football kickabout can be a nightmare for hens, a bit like living in a war zone. Chickens love peace, a place to work out their lives and pecking orders but if they are bombarded they get skittish and are far more likely to go off laying, become ill, fight, feather peck, cannibalise and attack people. A look at the life of a hen in a crowded chicken shed should give us some clues.

Chickens which are supposed to be free range but are actually in large sheds where there are thousands of birds with around an A4 sheet of paper each, are nervous creatures and there are frequent examples of aggressive behaviour between hens. If we inadvertently recreate the conditions of the chicken shed because there are children tearing around the garden all the time, the hens will not settle well. They will become nervous, shy away into dark corners, become more aggressive themselves and not do so well.

This doesn't mean that the children cannot play in the garden; they just have to respect their allotted spaces.

DISEASES

Avian flu

People envisage their chickens will pass on disease to their family. Talk about avian flu initially terrified the bird-keeping world, and then outraged it as the government suggested first that birds would have to be culled and then shut in.

The expected mass epidemic never really came and, generally speaking, outbreaks have been dealt with easily. These outbreaks come from wild bird populations, not poultry, so any outbreaks that do occur could appear anywhere. You are in no more danger of getting avian flu by keeping poultry than people that don't.

E. coli

It was Edwina Currie who set the cat amongst the chickens by famously saying that the UK poultry population was endemically infected with E. coli. This bacterium is responsible for dreadful digestive disorders that can kill. Children especially are susceptible to this problem.

It has to be said that the problem is still there and probably always will be because chickens do have a propensity to collect E. coli from their environment. But, and it is a big but, the bacterium settles mostly in the membranes between bone and meat. As long as the chicken is properly cooked, it is perfectly safe to eat. The only other possible route that the bacterium can get into people is via chicken poo.

Thankfully, this presents an excellent opportunity for education. Children can shift poo so long as they wear gloves and overalls and wash their hands afterwards. You need to get them into a regime of washing their hands whenever they handle the chickens, their litter or their eggs in any way. Thankfully, E. coli is not robust enough to cope with good soap and water.

And of course, as we have already shown, poultry can be immunised against it, so check with your supplier.

COPING WITH HORRID JOBS

There can be some horrid things to do when you keep chickens. With the best will in the world they are going to get red mite at some point in their lives, especially if you bring in birds from other flocks. They can get lice and so many other insect problems that might put children, especially children who are approaching teen years, right off the idea of keeping them.

Similarly, there is the eventual probability that you are going to have to cull, or at least get someone else to cull, your birds. This isn't a problem in itself, it is something that every pet owner has to think about, but most of the vets I have known have never been able to help when my hens were sick.

However poultry lice do not affect humans, so although they are pretty horrid in themselves, there is no worry about them infecting your children.

HOW TO KILL A CHICKEN

The needs of the commercial poultry grower are beyond the scope of this book, but we will briefly look at the law concerning killing of poultry.

When hens are killed for meat there is a three-stage-process involved. They are first attached, upside down on an overhead conveyor, and within a couple of seconds they are electrically stunned. This does not always kill the bird, but it does render it completely unconscious. Once stunned the bird feels no pain at all. Then a sharp blade is inserted in the mouth to cut the arteries of the neck and the bird slips into death without knowing a thing about it.

The law states that animals killed for meat have to be killed by a competent (licensed) person and that the animal has to be stunned before it is killed. The stun can be either percussive, using a bolt, or electrical.

There are no exceptions to this apart from two areas. The first is killing chickens for humane purposes. This takes the form of rapidly killing the hen by neck dislocation. The second is killing a single hen for personal consumption by the same method. The law is somewhat hazy about whether it is then legal to feed this hen to your family. Personal consumption has been interpreted by some as 'only by the person that killed it'.

The only other way it is legal to kill chickens – or any other animal for that matter – is by a free bullet. But you still have to be licensed if you want to then sell the carcass or the cooked meat.

What is absolutely sure is that you cannot keep hens, kill them yourself and cook them in a restaurant or farm café, or sell the meat in any way unless you are a properly accredited person with the right equipment and have gone through the various hoops required by trading standards and health inspectors.

But there are times when we have to kill a chicken either because it is sick, in too much pain or there are no veterinary services available.

What not to do

Don't chop the head off with an axe. This is a dangerous thing to do as far as the human is concerned. You get all worked up to do the job, the bird is held tightly and you chop not realising your finger is in the way. Secondly, you miss the neck and have to start again with a second blow, or a third and the worst case scenario is you have an injured bird, only seven fingers and a writ from the RSPCA.

Do not use a pole. A common method is to place a pole on the ground with a 'v' notch to take the bird's head. The bird is laid on the floor, the pole placed on the head in the appropriate place regarding the notch, and the feet are placed on the pole to hold it steady. The bird is then pulled backwards until the neck breaks. Frequently the head is pulled off. The bird isn't killed but just chokes or gets a severe strain of the neck.

Should you use a wall-mounted killer?

Some of you might find yourselves either disagreeing with this information or somewhat worried that you have one of these pieces of equipment. The concept of fitting a bird's head into what is essentially a pair of pliers is, to my mind at least, cruel. The bird feels pain as you pull the lever over its neck and there is stress involved in getting the bird in position in the first place. It is the stress question that makes me shy away from putting birds in one of those inverted 'killing cones' so popular in the USA.

How to kill a chicken by hand

Get someone to show you how to do this properly. Always treat the animal with the utmost care and respect.

This eventuality starts the very day you get chickens. Get them used to being handled, picked up and held firmly by the legs. This allows the bird to be completely stress free, even if you are completely stressed out because of what you are going to do. There is nothing wrong in killing a bird, especially if you do the very best and most caring job you can. It should be hoped that you will be able to do this job without any suffering on the bird's part.

Remember that if you are killing a sick animal you are doing it a good service. The alternative is to put the bird in a cage and take it either to another poultry keeper, or to a vet. Both of these involve time and discomfort, something the bird doesn't deserve.

The other aspect to all this is a moral one. You are not a barbarian by killing an animal in a humane manner. Get used to the idea that if you keep chickens there will be times when this is an important job of work.

If you get the opportunity, withhold feed for the last few hours, but not water, which should be freely available.

THE ACT

Pick the bird up and hold it firmly by the legs. Cup the head in the palm of the hands with the middle fingers pointing away from the beak, and the top of the head in the palm of the hand. Carefully and forcefully pull downwards on the head and twist. You will feel the bones break as the neck is severed. The bird now feels little or no pain because the messages are not getting to the brain. The bird starts to flap violently – this is a spasm and doesn't mean the animal is in pain. Within 15 seconds the bird is dead.

BREEDS

When you ask poultry fans what are the best chickens to keep, you are almost guaranteed a million different responses. You will often find that one person has never had a single problem with a particular breed but another has had a litany of difficulties with them.

I would say that from the outset you should not mix children who have never been in contact with poultry and rescue hens unless you are completely sure the children will behave quietly around them, at least until they have become used to their new surroundings and have regained their strength and stamina.

Of the breeds out there, and there are a lot of them, Silkies, Wyandotes and Buff Orpingtons are fantastic birds for the small family. They seem to chuckle along all day without any real problems and are friendly and robust. Warrens also seem to be quite happy amongst children. All these breeds give a good egg supply and are fairly clean in their habits.

Bantams and young children

An average chicken is a big animal to a five year old, comparable to an adult trying to cuddle an ostrich. So why not try keeping bantams which are smaller but in all ways the equal of their larger counterparts? Most large breeds have a bantam equivalent, and there are what is known as 'true' bantam breeds. Some bantam males can be quite aggressive but their small size makes them much easier to deal with. They lay quite prolifically and whereas the volume of a bantam egg is much smaller, the nutritional content is largely similar.

OTHER PETS

You might have the friendliest dog or the laziest cat in the world, but your hens will not know that. When first introduced your birds will have to be carefully protected for their own sake and know their runs and coops are secure. Do make your runs cat-proof by having netting over the top as well as the sides.

One of the more unpleasant aspects of keeping a dog is that they tend to urinate on everything and poultry find this unpleasant and intimidating to say the least. If your dog cocks his leg on the chicken house, keep him away, even if it means an extra fence around the coop and run.

Of course other wildlife will look at your birds with a hungry eye too. Most towns are heavily populated with foxes and unfortunately the stories of Mr Fox killing every chicken in the garden are quite true. Once he has found them he will return night after night. It is important that the hens are securely enclosed.

Rather magnificently, though just as deadly to the hens, the increase in raptors (birds of prey) in suburban areas has become a threat. I have seen chickens taken by sparrowhawks while eating on the ground and my neighbour's collection of pigeons has been attacked more than once.

SO, SHOULD I KEEP HENS?

The answer to that question is a resounding yes! There are difficulties, no one can deny it. Hens are a singular species and one that refuses to become domesticated on any other terms than its own. At times they display habits that are unpleasant and you have to have a good regime of cleanliness and care for the birds and your family. But the truth is that your lives will be enhanced beyond measure by the simple act of keeping poultry.

CHAPTER 2

ANATOMY OF THE CHICKEN

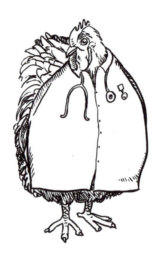

You do not need to know everything about the anatomy of the chicken in order to keep them, but an understanding of what is going on inside your bird will not only enhance the enjoyment and inform the keeper, it will also explain certain behaviour and provide hints to their care, or show what is happening when things start to go wrong.

SIMPLE CREATURES

Compared to mammals, birds are simple creatures. There are a number of structures that are unique to birds and some interesting organs that are there to make up for their lack of teeth. The hen's gut is a simple affair, and this is reflected in the way they get sick. Once you have a diet they thrive on, usually a mixture of plenty of grain in the form of layer's pellets or mash and plenty of foraging, then stick to it.

IMMUNITY

Another thing to bear in mind is just as the anatomy is simple, so is the immune system. The bird relies on its gut to provide it with all the resources it needs to keep a good level of disease resistance, and when the gut is impaired, either by incorrect feeding or by parasitic infestation, the bird can get sick. They can cope with two problems easily. Bad weather and mite infestation is just about within the limits of perseverance, but add to this poor feeding and the bird becomes sick very quickly.

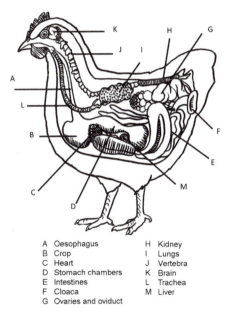

A	Oesophagus	H	Kidney
B	Crop	I	Lungs
C	Heart	J	Vertebra
D	Stomach chambers	K	Brain
E	Intestines	L	Trachea
F	Cloaca	M	Liver
G	Ovaries and oviduct		

The internal anatomy of the hen

EXTERNALLY

Comb and wattles

These are brilliant structures with multi function. In a way the female comb is like a light on the top of her head showing the cockerel she is ready to mate.

When at point of lay (POL) her comb flushes with blood and she gets plenty of attention from males. Similarly the comb is a sign for other females who are sure to be setting their affairs straight in maintaining the pecking order.

Birds do not sweat; rather they pant to control their body temperature. But the comb does provide some heat loss when the bird needs it.

The wattles are little 'combs' that hang from the cheeks. They were important for the ancestral hen as an orientation organ. They give the bird confirmation about its orientation when pecking.

Eyes

Chickens' eyes are on the side of the head and in order to make the best of forward vision they focus not by changing the shape of the lens, but by changing the shape of the cornea. This enables them to make the most of what forward vision they can get. Their eyes have greater acuity than human eyes. When you stand near to them they can see the fine detail of your clothing with greater sharpness. But they don't have good 3D vision, which is why they bob the head so they get an idea of the depth of objects by changing focus.

The eyelid is called the nicitiating membrane, which runs like a horizontal shutter. This needs to be moistened and enough water for the hen to wash its face, which it does from time to time, should be available in hot summers. Make sure it is cleaned out every day. There usually isn't any problem in the winter.

Beak

The chicken beak is more than just a horn-shaped hard mouth. The edge of the beak is lined with serrated edges allowing better grip, but the end of the serrations are fed with nerves so the animal can get a feeling for how hard it is biting, how delicate it is working and even how much care it needs when using the beak. An animal pecking at a chick is much more sensitive than one bashing a piece of oyster shell to pieces.

Ears

Chickens have two ears, below and behind the eyes, usually with an ear lobe on either side. You rarely have any problems with hen's ears, except sometimes lice.

Hackle, saddle and breast

The position just as the breast meets the neck, the tapering portion, is called the hackle. Sometimes these feathers are raised in fight situations (getting your hackles up!). The area behind this and over the back is called the saddle. When a particularly harsh cockerel pays too much attention to a hen she can get damaged in these areas, and any bleeding can in certain circumstances lead to feather pecking. This situation is eased by slipping a saddle over the bird like a bib, an otherwise ridiculous garment bought from some poultry suppliers.

The breast is towards the front and at the centre of the body and is disguised by the flight feathers.

Wing bar

These are brighter feathers on the wing, which cover the flight feathers. Sometimes they are more noticeable on pure breed birds, but they do reappear in offspring if you mate two hybrid birds.

Wings

The bone structure of the wing is almost identical to the human forearm, but clearly it is covered in feathers. Chickens do not fly any distance but do use their wings to gain height for roosting and to get over fences in order to make a nuisance of themselves. The power, as we have said, comes from the breast muscles.

Feathers

The end feathers, about ten, of the chicken's wing are the ones that provide the major thrust to send the animal skyward. They are the longest feathers on the wing. The secondary feathers are behind these and provide dome lift, but mostly make the shape of the wing into an aerofoil. When you clip the wing of the bird ONLY cut half way through the primaries well away from the base. If you cut too low, and near to the wing bone itself, the bird will bleed. It is likely to expire due to loss of blood! Only cut half way down one wing. This will unbalance the bird on takeoff and she will decide not to fly.

Shank, hock, spur and toes

The thigh of the bird's leg is hidden by the fluffy feathers that cover the lower half of the animal, but the lowermost knuckle, at the hock, is where the feathers end and the shank, covered with scales, begins. At the back of the leg below the hock is the spur, sometimes less visible in some breeds. The claws at the bottom have opposing 'toes' which are designed for gripping.

The difference between chicken wings and chicken legs

When we eat a chicken the legs are always large and the wings small. The meat on a chicken wing is disappointing whereas a drumstick is always welcome. However, in structural terms the muscle that drives the chicken wing is the whole of the breast muscle which we normally eat sliced. The muscle on the leg works the claw and the movement of the leg as a whole is powered by a large group of muscles that equates to the hip and buttock muscles in humans.

INTERNALLY

Breathing

Hens have smallish lungs inside a ribcage of seven pairs of ribs. However, they have no diaphragm. The lungs are attached to an interconnecting series of air sacs which in themselves are not associated with gaseous exchange, but act as a series of bellows to ventilate the lungs. In flight the action of flapping and other muscular movements in the bird is sufficient to maintain a steady stream of fresh air across the lungs.

The absence of a diaphragm makes the 'cleaning' or preparation of a chicken for cooking, much easier because you can easily remove the 'innerds' in one easy pull.

The lungs have another function: thermoregulation. Hot birds pant to evaporate water from the lungs, thus cooling them. Panting birds need to be put into the shade; too much sun can cause them problems. The nerves that control thermoregulation are in the neck, and as they pant this area can be cooled well below the actual body temperature, causing sunstroke.

The digestive system

Hens have no teeth and therefore food is broken up inside the body in an organ known as the crop, containing stones. The food is eaten and ground into a pulp by muscular action. It passes from here to the stomach where digestion starts. The various organs of digestion are familiar, the pancreas, the liver and the large and small intestines. Past the stomach there is a small amount of space for a long intestine, which ends in the cloaca.

The oviduct opens into the cloaca and eggs are pushed out of the single vent at the back end of the bird along with, but separately, faecal matter.

The crop

You can feel the crop on the chest of the bird more down to one side. It is a sack-like extension of the oesophagus. It is a muscular organ that has some small pebbles collected by the hen to help make slurry of the food she eats. Water is added and the food is ground. This process takes longer if the animal has been fed wheat or corn than pellets. Personally I feel the bird is improved from time to time if it is allowed a little corn. And you'd get pretty fed up if all you ate was mashed up food wouldn't you?

The stomach

This organ is also known by its southern United States sounding name as gizzard, but people in the UK often confuse this word with the crop. Absorption of sugars, the beginnings of protein digestion, all take place in the stomach or proventriculus. Digestive enzymes are secreted into the stomach where the first stage of chemical breakdown occurs. Water is absorbed in the stomach and some amino acids, but the majority of the food absorption takes place in the intestines.

People in China eat the hen's stomach, which isn't as bad as it sounds – we used to eat tripe in the UK.

Small intestine

The duodenum acts as the entry for the bile duct from the liver and the pancreas. Both organs have much the same function as in people. Bile emulsifies fats as well as being a waste product from the liver. The pancreas provides a cocktail of enzymes that acts directly on food and also provides insulin that moderates chicken metabolism.

Large intestine

This part of the chicken's anatomy is punctuated by two blind sacs called caeca. In a way these are similar to the human appendix, mostly on account of their apparent lack of use. I dare say they will be found to have some use in the hen, even if it is a place of incubation of the bacteria that populate the rest of the lower gut.

The large intestine is packed with bacteria that break down cellulose and the whole length of this part of the intestine reabsorbs water. Disease with this part of the animal brings with it the danger of dehydration.

Cloaca

This is the sewer of the hen, and the word 'cloaca' literally means sewer. It is a common space which both the oviduct and the intestine empties into, but in such a way that the eggs are not contaminated by the bird's waste.

As the egg is pushed out of the ovary and along its duct its presence pushes closed the large intestine and the cloaca becomes all oviduct. When the egg is not there, the chicken's own waste forces the oviduct portion of the cloaca shut, thus making it impossible for waste materials to enter the ovaries or their ducts.

The final part of the digestive system is called the vent – which you might refer to as the animal's bottom. It is a sphincter, which means it is made as a closable muscle.

The circulatory system

All birds have almost identical circulatory systems to humans. They have the same, four-chambered heart, which completely separates oxygenated and deoxygenated blood, essentially two circulatory systems with a single pump working them together. The chicken's heart is very efficient and consists of two atria at the top and two ventricles at the bottom. The system of arteries and veins is largely the same.

Liver

Of course these wonderful little organs, actually the largest in the hen's body, are so very tasty. Where would we be without pate? However, the liver is a very important organ for the living bird too, being the 'chemical factory' that metabolises most of the important substances a bird needs. The waste product of all this is called bile, which has a function in digestion.

Kidneys

Hens do have kidneys, even though they don't have a bladder. They drain into an area in the cloaca called the urodeum. Uric acid is made in the liver and is removed from the blood by the kidneys and this is vented out of the cloaca via the vent.

THE EGG FACTORY

The eggs in the ovary come in strings of cells where all the year's eggs are formed together for the year. When an egg is in production the germ cell is surrounded by yolk and albumen in its various forms (see Chapter 8). An outer membrane is randomly speckled with protein and at these sites the calcium carbonate is laid to make the shell. This process takes place as the egg moves along the oviduct and when the shell is ready the egg is laid.

Egg anatomy

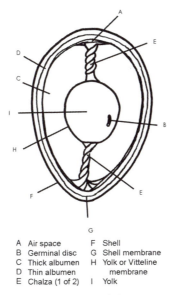

A Air space	F Shell
B Germinal disc	G Shell membrane
C Thick albumen	H Yolk or Vitteline
D Thin albumen	membrane
E Chalza (1 of 2)	I Yolk

The structure of the egg

Everyone knows the egg has three major parts: the shell, the white (or albumen) and the yolk. But there is much more to it than that; the egg is a complex structure and an understanding of what makes a good egg enhances our enjoyment of them.

Chicken eggs have a strong shell which is not airtight but which is less porous than most other eggs, ducks' eggs for example. The stronger the shell the better the egg keeps. You can improve their keeping by a month if you dip the shell in water glass, a silica-based liquid that has been used to preserve eggs for many hundreds of years. The silica clogs all the little holes and the egg stays fresh for longer.

Eggs in the fridge

There is a lot of debate, from time to time, about whether eggs should be kept in the fridge or not. After many years of extensive kitchen research I have found the best thing is to keep the eggs in the fridge, but bring them out into the kitchen to warm them up before use.

Eggs and disease

At one time everyone used eggs without worrying about their health status. A number of health scares have all but stopped this and we are extremely wary of diseases like salmonella. Today our stock should all be inoculated against disease, but we need to be sure when it comes to eating our own eggs.

If you have reared your own hens you need to be sure they are properly immunised at the proper stage, but we will look at this in more detail later.

I make it a rule never to eat uncooked eggs unless I am completely sure they are safe. It helps if you collect them as soon as practicable after they have been laid. Clean any faecal matter that might be on the shell and discard cracked eggs from the nest. Keep your eggs so that you eat them in order of laying. If you have only a few birds an egg skelter (a strong wire rack for storing eggs) is great fun. You load the eggs at the top and they roll down in turn towards the bottom as you use them.

Do not continuously handle eggs and make sure that you wash your hands before and after collecting them.

The chalaza

Two strands of white on either side of the yolk are simply there to support the yolk and stop it from settling against the shell. Where these are not present the egg could never mature to produce a chick. They are not a sign that the egg is going off.

The white (albumen)

This is full of protein and has two forms, the thicker around the yolk and the runny part nearer the shell. It ends at the inner shell membrane. An outer shell membrane lines the shell itself.

The yolk

The yolk is in the centre and has the germinal disc (sometimes you can't see it), which is the centre of fertilisation, and an outer membrane which is very fine indeed.

A note about breaking an egg: When you come to make fried eggs the most important thing is that the yolk stays intact. In order to ensure this, use the sharpest knife you can find and give the shell a careful but forceful tap. Don't bash it against the side of the pan. Then carefully empty the contents without splashing it with force. The vitelline membrane (the yolk membrane) will then not break.

An air sac at the blunt end of the egg is more a shock absorber to maintain the growth of the chick in its proper place than the provider of oxygen for life, which enters through the porous shell.

Contents of the egg

The egg is mostly water, around 75%, and around 11% of the whole weight of the egg is shell. Of the contents, the yolk is around 18% protein and nearly 33% fat, and the white is around 10% protein – the rest is water.

Of course there are also all the minerals and vitamins a young chick needs for all its developing life over the next few weeks.

Knowing a fresh egg

As an egg ages the air sack gets larger, and so you can use this to tell the freshness of an egg. If you place a fresh egg in cold water it will sink to the bottom and lay flat. If it floats a little, half way up, it is less fresh, and if it floats on the surface you should discard it.

In the pan a fresh egg sits up with a proud yolk and the white does not run away with itself all over the pan. You cannot tell the age of an egg by the colour of its yolk or the thickness of the shell. But you also need to keep a close eye on the shell quality and, if they are thin, provide more shell or chalk. Hen husbandry continues right until the egg hits the pan!

CHAPTER 3

BREEDS

WHY ARE THERE SO MANY DIFFERENT BREEDS OF CHICKENS?

As chickens were domesticated some ten or more thousand years ago, there are truly thousands of breeds. They have been our companions through the discovery and development of agriculture and so in all those years you would expect there to be quite a number of breeds. Breeds of chickens have been produced in order to balance four basic considerations.

Firstly, hens have been bred for improved egg production. The original hen laid maybe 50 eggs a year whereas the most modern breeds can lay 350 and even more.

Secondly, hens have been bred for meat production and over the years the speed at which the animal reaches a fair cooking weight has been important.

For many thousand years meat birds were cockerels thrown in the pot, but today they are specially bred.

Chickens somewhere between these two multipurpose birds that lay quite a few eggs, and yet at the same time have a decent amount of meat on them, have become popular amongst smallholders and urban poultry keepers. A side shoot of this idea has been the production of pigmy or bantam poultry, often complete miniature copies of bigger breeds, for ease of roosting. People often think that a bantam bird can cope with smaller living space. Well this might be true when it comes to roosting, but in fact they generally are more mobile, wider ranging and prefer more space than their larger cousins.

Susceptibility to disease and the ability to adapt to local climatic conditions have been other important considerations in cultivating breeds. When you consider that the original birds from which the modern chicken was bred came from the heat of the Middle and Far East, it is remarkable to see hens in all the climatic zones of the planet from the freezing poles to the sweltering equator.

Which birds are suitable for the back garden sometimes depends on exactly what you are going to do with them. Maybe you are looking for a garden slug remover, a few hens treated as pets and additions to the garden. Maybe you are looking for an egg-laying machine, or a bird that will be good for the table. Perhaps you have special needs for a bird that is particularly docile, quiet, small.

In reality you can keep any breed of chicken in a back garden or an allotment. Their general small size makes them reasonably easy to care for, but we shall have a look at the best animals for an urban lifestyle.

HOW TO BUY HENS

The popularity of poultry keeping these days is huge. Because of this there are dozens of companies who are queuing up for your custom, and the prospect of getting the right hen is sometimes daunting. These companies are easy to find in the poultry press, the smallholding press or on the internet. Particularly on the internet you can find all kinds of information as well as sources of poultry. It might be a good idea to try to find a few near you and visit them before you intend to buy. If you turn up and say you are contemplating keeping hens in the garden and ask for their advice, you can make a fairly informed judgement about which of them is the best breeder for you.

You can also take a friend with you who perhaps has hens of their own, but don't just accept any old advice. There is a tendency, particularly prevalent with popular pastimes, to be dogmatic and judgemental about who has what and unfortunately this is the case with some poultry keepers.

One of the problems a prospective purchaser of hens has to face is that individual breeds often have their names changed or shortened by their breeders. For example, what one breeder calls a Magpie Hen is actually a cross between a Barred Plymouth Rock and a White Rhode. This confusing state of affairs I feel is a little condescending to new poultry keepers, but then everyone has the right to name their own breeds. Keep your options open and don't just buy the first birds offered to you.

Breed societies

If you are going to buy pure breed hens there are breed societies (see Chapter 9 'Getting Help') who have control of the specification for the breed and a list of breeders. You are recommended to take this route, especially if the genetic authenticity of your birds is important to you. The same goes for rare breed poultry where, because there are so few of them, it is best to keep as pure a strain as possible.

Buying from auctions

Around the country there are a number of farm auctions that include poultry. They are almost all stocked by independent growers of one form or another, mostly small, one-man bands and even their children. You are faced with cage after cage of birds, some said to be one breed or another and they are almost always stressed.

Buying birds in these conditions is a bit of a lottery at best. You have no way of telling the age or health status of the birds in the cages, you cannot examine them for lice and you have no idea of when they were wormed, or if they were inoculated as chicks. You are buying almost blind.

For the birds this process is very stressful and it is in these conditions they both catch and succumb to diseases of all kinds so that when you get them home they might well become sick, just as a consequence of the way they were sold.

The same goes for buying eggs at auction. There is no saying if the eggs are what they say they are, you cannot candle them (check the inside of the egg for embryo growth by shining a light through it) or even handle them.

You are not able to return anything to the auction and there are no guarantees. So the answer is CAVEAT EMPTOR, which means 'buyer beware' but for me should read 'don't bother!'

It is much better to pay a little more and find a reputable supplier of healthy birds that have been inoculated and, well let's be honest, loved. And that is the best guarantee there is.

If you must buy from a market . . .

This is the only story in this book and I include it because it will show you what not to do. I have to admit this was my first ever contact with poultry, and I have learned my lesson, so don't write in complaining.

I went to Chelford market in Cheshire and loved the rows of sheep and cattle ready for sale. I had an allotment and on it was an empty chicken hut. I decided to fill it.

At the market poultry sale there were half a dozen people bidding for cages of birds and so did I. I won a few, and was very pleased too, but I didn't actually know what I had bidded on. In total I spent very little money, about £20.

I paid my money and went to collect my winnings. In cages there were an assortment of rabbits, three cockerels and a couple of very large birds that looked to me to be asleep. These were transferred to pet boxes and put in the back of the estate car.

The journey home was a nightmare. The birds started to pant, so I opened the sunroof to let some air into the car, although the windows were open. Stopping at the traffic lights we were alarmed to see a cockerel (he always was a cheeky one) land on the bonnet and eyeball me. Goodness knows how he escaped, I still haven't worked it out! In the time it took the lights to turn to green the animal had decided to hop on the top of the car and in through the sunroof. He sat on the back seat and pooed, but there he stayed for the rest of the journey.

Needless to say the hens were useless. They had a happy life but never gave me a single egg. There has to be a better way of buying hens.

Buying point of lay pullets

The term point of lay is a bit of a misnomer. You might think that they are more or less ready to lay eggs straight away, but this partly depends on the time of year they were hatched, the weather, their feeding regime and so on. It can be a frustratingly long time before a point of lay pullet actually decides to start laying.

A hen can come into lay any time between four and eight months, though both these extremes are questionable. The first signs of a hen ready to lay include the following. Her comb will flush, turning from a very pale colour to a blushed pink – literally the light on the top of her head switching on. This is normally a couple of weeks before she starts to lay. The pelvic bones open out – well they have to pass an egg – and if you can get two fingers between them by the rude but not unpleasant act of pushing the fingers near the vent at the back, the bird is not that far from laying. She also starts to eat more voraciously.

The only thing you can say about a so-called point of lay bird is that she is approaching five months of age.

PURE BREEDS AND HYBRIDS

All birds are extremely good at interbreeding. You only have to look at the wide variety of so called 'mallards' on the duck pond to realise that hybridisation is one of the ways that birds maintain their genetic vigour. Humans have used this to their advantage to cross poultry of different strains to produce animals with the best characteristics of both parents. Biologically speaking there is no such thing as a pure breed chicken. They have all been bred from some other breeds in the past and then bred again to keep them suitable for modern times. A pure breed hen is one that breeds true to type and has been recognised as an independent type.

PURE BREEDS

These are strains of poultry that have been developed over many years to breed true. That is a cockerel and a hen of the type will always produce nothing but the same type of hen or cock. These pure breeds might, many years ago, have been the result of a hybrid cross, but have been consistently chosen over many generations to produce male and females that are alike and breed true.

One of the difficulties of this process is that over many generations you might be selecting characteristics that have an important affect on another characteristic of the bird. For example, some breeds were at one time excellent layers but over the years this has fallen off because breeders arbitrarily chose to breed from birds with the neatest combs. The neater the comb the fewer eggs the bird produced. This is because of the way the unseen genetics of the animal affects other characteristics.

Modern breeding is not anything as haphazard and new breeds should last a lot longer than some of the old ones.

For the urban poultry keeper there are many pure breed birds that are worth having either because they lay well, grow into excellent table birds or simply look pretty. The choice is yours, it's your garden!

PURE BREEDS FOR THE GARDEN

There are hundreds of pure breed hens, but here we stick to those best for the garden. All hens are divided into groups, soft feathered or hard feathered, true bantams and rare breed. The soft-feathered birds are further divided into light or heavy types. On the whole, heavy birds are not the best for the garden for a number of reasons. Firstly they are not so good at laying, being generally meat birds. The majority of urbanites (and I include myself in this) are really interested in egg production over meat, so you need a good layer.

Ancona

This is a compact, striking bird developed in Italy in the 1830s and spread from there around the world by 1900. It is black and white and has bare orange legs. It needs little space really, but is also a hot tempered bird. They do not take to being handled and cocks can tend to fight most things including humans. The Ancona produces smallish eggs and in a way resembles a large bantam bird – although there is a bantam version. The Ancona produces around 170 eggs a year. This bird is handsome and a great garden forager but needs a little expert handling from time to time, whenever they get flighty.

Black Rock

This is a brilliant garden hen. For a start they can cope with being left alone so long as they have adequate food and water. Their feathers are robust and thick, offering excellent protection to the elements. They are chunky little hens, keeping themselves warm in any number of climates and have plenty of hybrid vigour. The eggs are a uniform decent size and have very strong shells. If you are going to keep poultry in exposed high altitude where the wind and rain

competes with the chill to make winter miserable, then the Black Rock is for you.

Genetically, the Black Rock is a cross between the Rhode Island Red and the Barred Plymouth Rock. They are black with some chestnut markings and they produce brown eggs, around 230 of them a year.

Orpington

This bird has been developed in Kent. It is all feathers and comes in buff, black, white and blue, but it is the buff type that is the most popular.

It is an extremely docile bird that doesn't mind being picked up, will be friendly towards children and basically bok bok its way through life very happily. They lay around 140 to 160 eggs in their first year and aren't as big as they look really. They have a tendency to get a bit messy in the rain, and are showy, pampered-looking pets.

For all that, they are not too good with other breeds, especially flighty ones, and you have to be careful to avoid outbreaks of feather pecking.

Because of its size you should consider very carefully the size of the housing needed to keep three or four birds as a minimum.

Leghorns

I don't know why but I always feel the Leghorn is a fighting bird. Of course it isn't; many docile hens wear spurs. Leghorns come in many colours and sizes but all of them have large combs, red eyes and white earlobes. Their wattles are long and rounded and they have firm bodies. They are fairly compact birds which lay well.

They are excitable animals and get spooked easily, especially if your household is noisy. They don't mind being confined to a small run, but because they are small they are good at flying. Their large combs bring problems. They need more food in the winter to 'pay' for the heat loss and they do tend to have problems with fighting and generally catching it about the garden.

Leghorns have one thing in their favour: they eat more slugs than any bird I know!

Plymouth Rock

This isn't from Devon, but the USA where it was developed in the 1820s. It comes in two colours, white or buff, and is a big bird so small housing is out of the question. There is also a barred variety with red comb and white wattles. It was developed as a dual-purpose bird that gave a reasonable supply of eggs and yet also a good carcass for the table.

The Plymouth is probably the best bird to have children around because they are so docile, easily tamed, can be handled easily and they are robust. They are the probably the safest birds to allow the freedom of the garden, but they also have a tendency to put on weight unless they get adequate exercise. They will give around 150 to 170 eggs a year.

Wyandottes

These are somewhat delicate-looking birds but are fantastic layers, giving over 200 in the first year. They are also generally compact and pretty birds that do well in the garden. They are good with children and other pets, not being phased much by anything.

They come in all shades and colours – white, black speckled, silver speckled – and are much alike in habit and temperament. They are named after a tribe of North American Indians.

They are particularly happy in a confined run and make excellent garden pure breeds.

Rhode Island Red

These were the birds my family kept from the war and right through my childhood. I remember playing football with a big cockerel, I would kick the ball to him and he would push it around the garden back to me (eventually).

They are great hens, sturdy and robust, and love to walk around in a flock, pecking and scratching about. They come in large and bantam forms, and are prolific layers – around 200 a year. The large ones are big birds, so housing should be thought about carefully.

They are very forgiving birds and will put up with all kinds of surroundings, and respond to care with lots of eggs and a happy gait around the garden.

Brahma

Included because it is such a striking bird, the Brahma makes a fantastic show in the garden. Let's face it, many people have gardens that are supposed to look good and this animal is just like a bunch of flowers. It will certainly impress the neighbours too.

It is easily handled and quite docile and has just the right temperament for the garden. As well as being easily handled, it is fairly self-contained and just gets on with life. They will never be your best friend, they won't come running for food, but they won't be your worst enemy either.

They need a larger hut to sleep in, especially if you are going to run more than one bird – which is a fairly important requirement. They are not fantastic layers, giving about 140 eggs a year.

The major problem with them is their feathered legs. They need to be cleaned well and de-loused and they must be kept dry.

Sussex

These birds look like chickens! They are large and soft feathered and come in lots of colour variations. They are always on the go, looking into everything, and they seem not to be worried about people or pets. They also do well in a run. They have a lot of eggs, well over 200 a year. They are altogether a brilliant bird to keep.

Maran

This is an excellent garden bird, hovering up slugs all day long. They come in different colours but the most popular is the speckled cuckoo variety. They can get aggressive and are not too happy being handled or generally messed with. They can peck, as my thumb will testify! Otherwise they make great garden birds, if not pets, and will easily augment their ration with garden pests. They have around 180 eggs in the first year and the shells are a dark brown colour.

Barnevelder

These are the most beautiful birds, as Gerard Manley Hopkins says, 'Praise God for dappled things!'. I totally agree. The Barnevelder is the most beautiful dappled bird that will melt the heart of any neighbour looking at them.

This is possibly the best hen for the garden you can get (though I have said that about other hens), as it is not only docile, it isn't that worried about things either. Inquisitive and friendly, a group of four or so will forage around the place with great interest. Egg number is on the low side but they are big and brown and wonderfully tasty.

Welsummer

The Welsummer just looks like a contented hen. They come in large and bantam sizes and as such gives you the impression of graceful calm. A proper lady, she is completely docile, doesn't mind being picked up, and is an excellent bird to share the garden with children.

They produce around 150 eggs a year with a dark brown shell. They mix well with other birds too, so is great for a mixed flock in a small garden.

Marsh Daisy

Rare but lovely is the best way to describe this bird, but they're here because they come from my neck of the woods. The hens are golden, from greyish at the vent to lovely yellow at the head, and they are a pleasure to have around. They are generally fine amongst people but can get a little nervous where there is a lot of noise. You can be sure they are safe birds for children to be near and they lay a bit too – around 160 a year.

New Hampshire Red

This is another American bird that in many respects resembles the Rhode Island. They are soft feathered and hardy birds that don't mind being picked up by children (and occasionally dropped) and they are quite used to wet, cold conditions. There is a newly created bantam version too.

They produce a lot of eggs, some reports pre-War said more than 300, but I would suggest half that is more like the norm.

Australorp

This bird was developed in Australia and is wonderfully black/green in colour. It has a lot of Black Orpington in it and is a very useful dual-purpose bird, laying around 200 eggs a year and giving plenty of meat too. It is a good family chicken; excellent with children and doesn't mind being handled. Unphased by pets or other chickens, the Australorp might well be a good bird for someone who is beginning to take their poultry keeping to a higher level because they make excellent mothers.

This is one of those animals that, as a result of selecting hens for a black coat, has had its egg laying abilities diminished somewhat.

PURE BREEDS UNSUITABLE FOR THE URBAN SITUATION

You might disagree with the following advice if you happen to be a keeper of a certain breed. Some of the reasoning behind my comments might seem harsh to you. My only answer is, fantastic! If you are successfully keeping the following birds in the city, all the better.

The game breeds

Birds like the Indian Game, Old English Game and so on are smallish, flighty birds that are both aggressive and noisy. The males will fight, often to death, and they simply hate being confined. They are genetically close to the old cock fighting birds, and they don't lay many eggs.

Cochin

You might want to keep a Cochin, though for me it is too feathery, doesn't lay well and is best for the exhibitors to lavish their love and attention on.

Dorking

This is a lovely bird that is excellent for the table. Its egg laying abilities, however, aren't that good and they do not like being confined that much, so if you have only a small space available it simply will not be happy.

Silkie

This bird is so lovely to look at; they resemble ostrich chicks that are destined never to grow up. But the nature of the feathers makes them hard work, especially when everything starts to get muddy.

HYBRID BIRDS

People have, and thankfully still do, cross breeds of chickens to make more fertile, more adaptable and better suited chickens. After a while the genetic success is watered down by generations of breeding. Take the New Hampshire as an example. There are reports of them laying an egg a day for a year in the 1930s, but the same breed does not produce anything like that many these days. So hybrid hens are constantly the order of the day for many reasons, not always good.

Hybrid hens are developed for fast growth to take a bird from hatching to table weight in 12 weeks, and that cannot be a good thing for hen welfare. But a hybrid hen that is docile, designed to lay a reasonable number of eggs on a small amount of food, and that happily wanders around the garden can only be a good thing. We have to remember that all hens, like most farm animals, are somehow human-made by selecting the parents with characteristics that seem useful to us. Most people would not want to keep truly wild hens, and neither should they.

If I were to come right out with it and suggest a hen for the new keeper or for one in a very urban situation, the ordinary commercial brown hybrid (such as Warrens or Speckledy Hen) is the ideal. They have all the characteristics of an excellent urban hen: good layer, good temperament and easy to manage.

They actually do better if they are let out in the morning, provided with adequate water and food, shade and security and then totally ignored until the evening when they are shut up for the night. Notwithstanding, they need their clean outs and treatments for lice too, but on the whole they are perfectly happy to live their own lives while we live ours.

Warrens

This is the brown/red hen that tends to live by the thousands in battery houses. They lay around 320 eggs a year, so you can see how much improved the hybrid is compared to the pure breed. That said, Warrens are perfect hens for the garden too. In a way they look like the Rhode Island Red's poor relation, but have a docility and vigour that in fact far outstretches them. They don't fly much, are easily caught, can be petted by children and have a generally good resistance to disease.

Their cost makes them the most economical happy little hen you will find.

You only get females since they will not breed true. Any males do not resemble the females and are easily removed.

Speckledy Hen

This is a cross between the Rhode Island and the Maran, and you get a really pretty bird that gives around 270 eggs a year. This is also a docile, good urban bird and the eggs are brown. In general the darker the eggs the fewer you get, so 270 is a huge number for brown eggs!

Miss Pepperpot

This is a three-way hybrid. That is to say it is the result of crossing a Rhode Island Red with another hybrid – a cross between a Maran and a Plymouth Rock. This is also an excellent garden bird, a prolific layer of enormous brown eggs.

It is one of the modern hybrids that have all kinds of fancy names, but this particular type is only available as a female.

Gingernut Ranger

This is another modern hybrid of a Rhode Island Red and a Sussex. This particular cross shows another aspect of hybridisation called sex linkage, which also explains why no Pepperpot males are available.

Sex linkage

If you cross a Rhode Island Red male with a Light Sussex female, you will find the offspring are different according to sex. All the females look a little like the cockerel – the Rhody. The males look like their mother. This is sex-linked inheritance and some strains of one of the sexes are not viable at all and do not appear. Sex linkage makes the chicks of such crosses easy to segregate because the males are light and the females are dark.

BATTERY HEN WELFARE TRUST HENS

The Battery Hen Welfare Trust (BHWT) is an organisation that takes poultry from intensive poultry farms once they have had their first run of eggs and are less economic. No poultry farm wants to feed hens that are in moult because they don't produce any eggs. So a number of them donate their birds to the trust. They are invariably the brown Warren type hybrid that might be in lay still, but are most probably moulting. There are a number of similar trusts around the country, but the BHWT is the biggest.

You have to make contact (you can find your nearest representative on their website: www.bhwt.org.uk) and book your birds. They usually cost a nominal fee, but that isn't the point. You will pay much more in care than the value of the money.

People new to keeping poultry should think carefully about the consequences of getting birds from this route. Almost invariably they are healthy animals, but going from the confines of a battery cage to the great open spaces (to them) of a chicken run is a huge step and it is not uncommon for them to die.

They can get sick just by the shock of a new regime or by the sudden influx of intestinal parasites, which they can get if put on infected land, or they can be bullied if run with other hens. The cost of treating this sickness might be a lot more than the value of the hens. They are not going to be cheap birds, and neither should they be thought of in that way.

Introduce these birds to an existing run carefully. Keep them separate if you can for a week but so that they can see each other. Make sure your other birds are treated for lice and there is no red mite in the hut. Then gradually introduce them, but watch out for trouble, especially if you have any males.

Probably, all will go well and your introduction will be trouble free. Once they get used to running about the likelihood is your rescue hens will be at least as prolific and healthy as any bird you have.

BREED CHECKER

Pure breeds	Characteristics	Broodiness	Temperament	Number of eggs	Colour of eggs
Ancona	Black and white	Not much	Can be flighty	170	Cream
Australorp	Black with green tinge	Reasonably good mothers	Docile	180–200	Light brown
Barnevelder	Beautiful copper laced	Not quick to go broody	Easily bullied	160–180	Dark brown
Black Rock	Brilliant black birds, can have golden chests	Not great broodies	Easy care, quite friendly actually	260–280	Brown
Brahma	Gorgeous golden, red and black big birds	Go broody easily, good mothers	Easy to handle but don't mix well, can be bullied	130–150	Brown
Leghorns	Look somewhat like the French Hen – big comb	Do not go broody	Can be noisy, get excited and run around. Not good with pets	180–200	White
Maran	Look like a pepper pot, black/grey	Not easily broody	Can be aggressive	180	Dark brown
New Hampshire Red	Look like the big red hen, reminiscent of Rhode Island Red	Easily broody, good mothers	Completely docile, if left alone. Will defend themselves at a push	120–140	Brown
Orpington	Big, orange, lovely hens	Not easily broody but make good mothers	Easy to handle but can be bullied by other breeds	150–170	Brown
Plymouth Rock	Buff, dark cream or white – big birds	Not easily broody but make good mothers	Easily handled and petted	160 large eggs	Light brown

Pure breeds	Characteristics	Broodiness	Temperament	Number of eggs	Colour of eggs
Rhode Island Red	Medium-sized to large, nut brown birds with darker neck feathers. Brilliant red comb and wattles	Don't go broody often	Self-contained, happy anywhere, easily handled	200 plus	Brown
Sussex	Handsome large bird, buff and gold	Goes broody easily in second year	Excellent bird, easy to handle and great to watch	180–220	Light brown
Welsummer	Golden Russet, laced with soft feathers beneath	Not broodies and poor mothers	Friendly birds, good for children	140–160	Dark red brown
Wyandotte	White with black neck and tail. Striking medium-sized birds	Reasonable in second year, possibly third	Can cope in almost all weathers and easily cared for	180–200	Light brown

Hybrid breeds	
	All the hybrids will give you 300 eggs a year at least. They are almost all uniformly brown/red except for Miss Pepperpot and Speckledy Hen. They do not go broody and in many cases you can only get females.
Brown Commercial	Usually the eggs are brown and large in size.
Gingernut Ranger	They don't particularly mind being kept in small runs and tend to put up with children and pets reasonably well. They don't really like being repeatedly handled.
Miss Pepperpot	
Speckledy Hen	
Warrens	

74

CHAPTER 4

FEEDING YOUR CHICKENS

Hens are funny creatures. They resemble humans in a way because they have a definite regime of feeding, cleaning, going off foraging and sleeping. They take themselves off to roost at night and take a few minutes to get themselves going in the morning. So long as they have plenty of good food and clean water along with adequate pasture to roam in and shelter, they will remain very happy and live a potentially full life.

However, in their preferred food they do not particularly resemble humans. They can be prone to cannibalism, particularly if they happen on a broken egg when they will compete to get their share.

NO TEETH

As we have already seen in Chapter 2, chickens have no teeth. They eat small pieces of grit which remains in the crop and is used to smash the food to a

A grit hopper

paste before it passes along the gut. You can buy hard grit for hens from your local supplier.

Oyster shell is used to give the birds the calcium and carbonates they need to make eggshell. Crushed oyster shell is an important part of the diet and they peck at it all day. I have found it best to provide it in two ways: in a tray so they can just go to it once they know it's there and scattered around so they can just happen on it when they are scratching about.

THE HEN'S DIGESTIVE SYSTEM

On the whole, the poultry digestive system is simple. Being omnivores they eat animal and vegetable matter. But this doesn't mean they can easily eat human-type food. They don't do well on bacon bits and pieces of sausage, but much prefer insects, spiders and worms.

Essentially they have to use the few short inches from beak to cloaca to extract from their food all the proteins, minerals, carbohydrates and all the water they need to live. It is quite an intensive process.

The beak can break food into easily swallowed pieces and that's all. They do not chew at all, but instead make a paste in their crop, which is at the base of the neck. This is a muscular sack where food, stones and water are churned together to make a paste.

Food can remain in the crop, which is little more than a sack in the oesophagus and little digestion takes place there. When the animal is ready the paste is transported into the stomach where the food is digested more readily.

The stomach (or proventriculus) is where protein and carbohydrate digestion takes place. From there, the food slurry passes into the duodenal loop where it is mixed with bile and enzymes from the pancreas for the digestion of fats and further digestion of starch.

The duodenal loop passes food into the small intestine where the various nutrients are absorbed into the bloodstream and from there to the liver to complete the chicken's metabolism. The waste material is passed to the large intestine where some cellulose is absorbed in the caeca, which resembles our appendix. Poultry cannot really cope with lots of roughage, so don't bother feeding it to them! The large intestine also reabsorbs water from the remains of the food before it is egested.

The cloaca, which literally means sewer, has a complicated double stopping anatomy making it unlikely that faecal material can contaminate the reproductive system, which also vents to the cloaca.

RECOGNISING GOOD CHICKEN POO

It is important to know when a chicken is off colour, and one of the ways you can do this is to compare their droppings from day to day. It is well worth becoming an expert on chicken poo because this will provide you with umpteen clues about your hen's health.

If you took some brown cardboard and chewed it up, rolled it into a very small cigar, painted a bit of it white and then curled it over itself, this would look like the ideal dropping. It should be fluffy, solid-ish, not runny and white in parts. Hens do not have a bladder and their urine is a white substance found in the poo. This white is sometimes referred to as urates, and consists of a high concentration of uric acid.

Chicken poo shouldn't look like a white inner surrounded by a clear liquid as though it was a strange egg. It shouldn't be yellow and runny.

Reasons for runny poo

- Too much protein
- Parasitic infestation
- Change in diet/environment
- Sickness (we will return to this topic later)

It stands to reason that there should be no blood in the poo and there should be no obvious discomfort when the bird is at its business.

HOW TO FIND A LOCAL SUPPLIER OF HEN FEED

Living in a big city brings many benefits; there are so many shops, but not that many agricultural suppliers. The company that sold you your chickens will probably have a supply of feed, but it isn't always either the most convenient nor the cheapest place to buy from. Shopping around might provide a better alternative, especially if you can look on the internet.

Should you be unable to find poultry suppliers, try pigeon fanciers suppliers, which is still a very urban pastime and still fairly widespread. They often stock poultry feed and, if they don't, they invariably know someone that does.

RATIONS FOR LAYING HENS

There are a number of different feeding regimes for which a pre-formulated feed is available. You wouldn't expect chicks to feed from the same dish as their mother hen, and neither would you expect a growing bird to have the same nutritional requirements as a laying hen.

For now we will look into the layer's ration designed for a hen at point of lay and into her laying period. The specific requirements of chicks and growing birds will be dealt with in other chapters.

What the food has to do

A laying bird has a lot of food requirements. It needs to keep the bird warm, so in cold weather the birds will eat more. This is particularly important in hard frosts where the birds will benefit from an evening feed of hard maize (corn). This takes time to digest and makes the birds hot – well hotter than normal.

Secondly the feed has to provide everything the animal needs to maintain the correct working of the metabolism – particularly the immune system. On top of this the animal has to digest its food, make oils, blood, everything it needs. Then, of course, it is producing eggs and therefore needs an adequate supply of protein, fat and calcium.

Layer's ration

The most common way of feeding laying poultry is with pelleted ration. The pellets are made of wheat for carbohydrates and therefore energy, soya bean pulp for protein and various supplements, essential oils, minerals and vitamins. They can also include medication, which is usually used by commercial farmers, but non-medicated food is widely available.

Laying birds are fed a ration that is 16% protein, and this comes mostly from soya, but can also be provided in the form of fishmeal. As well as pellets, mash is also available which basically contains the same ingredients from which pellets are made. Mash used to be the major way of feeding poultry but it is not easy to put in hoppers and the battery hen farmers also wanted to get more food into hens more quickly than them having to peck away at mash.

Hens do not over eat once they have their daily ration, which is about 120 g or 4 oz. This can be stored in a hopper which either hangs or sits on the floor. In the city, if you use such a method it is a good idea to remove the hopper at night so that rats are not attracted – so long as you put it back the following morning. Alternatively use a trough, which again can be emptied at night. This might seem like a great imposition, but it's a chore worth keeping to in the urban situation.

Organic?

You can buy ordinary grade pellets or organic grade pellets and there are also a number of lower protein crumb-type mixtures that all can be used in hoppers or otherwise. The lower protein feed is a response to birds having runny droppings, but if you are feeding a high volume layer hybrid, you might wish to keep to the 16% protein feed, after all you only get out what you put in.

A new range of feed is available specially designed for ex-battery hens, which has a little extra protein but a lot more essential oils and vitamins.

SUPPLEMENTING THEIR DIET

There is a lovely World War II book, recently reprinted, called *Keeping Poultry and Rabbits on Scraps* by Claude Goodchild and Alan Thompson. The problem when we were at war was that grain was important for human consumption and they rationed the birds with only 60 g or 2 oz a day. This wasn't enough, so the chicken keeper had to augment this ration with other foods such as greens, boiled potatoes and so on.

Today, if you look at the government regulations, it is more or less illegal to feed any scraps to chickens, or any other animal for that matter. The laws are in place to combat transfer of disease, particularly foot and mouth in pigs, but also strains of virus and salmonella in chickens. If you are selling your eggs you have to prove that any feed other than official pellets has been grown for the chicken's own use, and not mixed chicken/human use. So the practice of removing the outer leaves of a cabbage for the hens and using the inner part of the vegetable for the household dinner is, strictly speaking, illegal.

The important thing is to give extra food in the afternoon, so the hens will consume their pellet ration first. The extra food is shredded into small pieces where possible or cooked when it is something like potatoes. It is important that the food is never there to replace the pellet ration and that there is nothing left hanging around to attract vermin.

Vegetables

Hens will eat vegetables with great delight. They are not good with onions but will consume garlic, which is said to help their digestion. It is a major constituent of certain health preparations for poultry and other livestock. There is some literature that suggests feeding garlic to hens actually increases their egg laying, but this has not been tested scientifically and to be honest it is difficult to see how this can happen.

It is fun to watch hens feeding on vegetables dangling on a string from above. This works particularly well with a cabbage and they play pecking at it, making it swing. Don't let any vegetables rot in the run, once they look as though they have had enough, take it away. An alternative is to shred the food into small pieces, making it easy to feed and eat.

The important thing is that any extra food is given in the afternoon, so the hens will consume their pellet ration first. Supplemental food is never given to replace the pellet ration and you should have nothing left hanging around to attract vermin.

Supplement mash

A recipe for incorporating vegetables into the diet includes boiling up vegetables, carrot tops, potato peelings, almost anything as long as it can be made to go 'mushy', then straining and mixing the vegetables with layers mash, which will serve to dry the vegetables off.

There are lots of recipes, most of which are fine in moderation so long as you don't expect to save corn ration and you don't boil up mashes with salt. Hens are very susceptible to salt, much more than we are. For this reason it is not a good idea to feed them products prepared for human consumption and certainly titbits like crisps and chocolate are definitely out of the question.

A MASH RECIPE FOR TWO HENS

You can multiply this recipe for more hens if you like. I prefer to make a fresh batch of this once a week and leave it for the hens to eat for only two days, removing the waste to the compost heap.

You need:

  2 potatoes, not peeled but cut into small pieces

  A handful of porridge oats

Finely chopped greens of any type

A chopped clove of garlic

Simply boil the vegetables until they are soft and then pour out most of the water, saving a little for the oats to soak up. Chop up all the vegetables into a rough mash with a knife and then add the oats. You are looking to keep the mash moist but not runny.

Allow this to cool and then serve in a bowl that you can remove at night. After two days they don't seem to eat any more of it, so I compost the remains.

Other feed supplements

There are on the market various tonics and preparations designed to keep your poultry healthy. On the whole I have to say that the main thing for poultry is a wholesome hen ration in the morning and other interesting feeds for the rest of the day, which give variety more than anything else. Keeping them clean and parasite free is another important aspect of hen care. From time to time it is necessary to worm them and the added feed supplements, usually formulated from garlic and natural oils of one kind or another, do not do this completely. Some people swear by their supplements; others have had bad experiences. So I suppose it is down to choice. I choose not to use them, but that's just me!

THE COMPOST BOX

If your hens are free ranging they will make a bee-line for the compost if available. This is because it is usually full of beetles and worms, not to say the odd frog and newt. They love to scratch around and collect food, and you can almost see their delight. If your birds are not free ranging and live in a run, provide them with a shallow tray, as large as possible, and from time to time provide them with the treat of a few spades of compost for them to peck about in. Sure enough, they will manure this compost and what is left after a day or so can be returned to the heap.

In an urban situation it is best to be as secure as you can be when it comes to providing extra food. Do not just throw vegetables willy-nilly into the pen and be sure the food is always cleared away at the end of the day. Of course, in a wider, more open aspect, say of the allotment, there is more leeway when it comes to throwing weeds and spent vegetables into the pen for pecking.

I have found that hens adore brussels sprouts to peck at, so if you have any exploded ones, let the birds have them.

WATER

It goes without saying that water is vital and they should never be without it. Freshen the water every couple of days, don't let it languish in the hot sun and

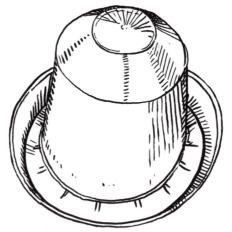

An upturn water reservoir

make sure it is always clear. Don't force them to drink soiled water. A healthy hen will drink at least a pint a day, so it is surprising how quickly it goes down.

GRIT

Hens need to have tiny pebbles and pieces of smooth rock in their crops to help break the pieces of food into pulp, increasing the efficiency of digestion. This is often picked up in the run, but it can be bought specially for the hens to peck at. Chicks fed on chick or grower's mash do not need grit at all, unless they are eating whole grains. You can buy special chick grit, but it is probably better not to feed them anything other than bought chick or grower's mash.

The difference between chick mash and grower's mash

Chick mash (also known as chick crumbs) is simply rolled mashed grains that are small enough and soft enough for the bird to swallow easily. They provide all the carbohydrates and proteins the birds need. Chick mash is fed dry and is around 22% protein, far too much for adult birds. If you have a broody hen with them, provide her with her own feed separately. After around six weeks they can be fed the next stage, grower's pellets (or grower's mash). These contain slightly less protein, though still too much for an adult, and they should be slowly introduced to the new feed over a week or so.

OYSTER SHELL

Laying hens need a lot of calcium and other minerals in order to make all those shells. Their feed ration does contain calcium but it is better to supplement this with some calcium carbonate in the form of ground oyster shell, which is easily absorbed by the hen. This will top up the bird's blood levels and thus produce good, strong eggshells.

You can buy the correct oyster shell and this should be simply available for the hens to peck at in a bowl.

SHOULD I USE A HOPPER?

Hoppers allow hens to peck freely at their food without the need for you to have to replenish it daily. Pellets are specifically designed for feeding from a hopper. Most hoppers have a lid and keep the food dry and free flowing. This is a super method for when you have more than a couple of birds and where rats are not perceived to be a problem.

In a true urban situation you need to be sure you are not leaving food around for rats to find and, possibly more importantly, for people to be able to imagine rats can easily get at. For this reason I always recommend that for a couple of hens a simple bowl is an excellent solution. They can be placed on a tray or board and completely removed to a secure position at night time, to be returned when you open the hutch in the morning.

Small dish hoppers can be removed each night

If you are using a hopper, place it over a tray so that spillages do not simply fall into the grass, and you can remove this too.

CANNIBALISM

Hens are not humans and they will eat their chicks in certain circumstances. They love eggs too, and will run across the garden to fight for a dropped egg. Try not to let these things happen as they can lead to other problems. If hens get a taste for eggs they might also start to feather peck and bully other bids. Part of the problem with feather pecking is the taste of blood which will invariably flow from the inflicted animal. Always keep chicks and the rest of the flock apart until they are big enough to fend for themselves, which usually means more or less at the point of lay.

POINTS TO REMEMBER

Feed a basic 120 g (4 oz) ration of bought layer's pellets or mash

- Give plenty of water

- Clear away food at night and store away from vermin

- 'Extras' such as cooked vegetables can be given in the afternoon

- Do not give any other human food. (They don't like crisps!)

- Let them scratch for their own food

- Provide grit and crushed oyster shell

- Avoid letting them taste eggs or blood

CHAPTER 5

POULTRY CARE

The urban hen brings with it a series of responsibilities which, in some cases, are more onerous than the country hen. Some of these responsibilities have already been referred to elsewhere in this book, but are important enough for a second mention here. It is best if you attack the chores of poultry keeping in a methodical way, splitting the jobs into daily, weekly and monthly tasks. Hens get on best when left alone to do whatever they do, but in order for you to get the most out of them, and to keep them in tip top condition, you have to spend time with them.

You will not find better companions for a quick natter and they are perfect for that one-way conversation we all need now and then. I used to talk to my bees when I didn't have any hens, but they frequently disagreed with me in the most violent way.

DAILY JOBS

The morning routine is possibly the most important because it is set by you. Once used to what you do the birds adapt easily, but you must stick to it. If you let the birds out at 7 am, it must be more or less 7 am every day. Otherwise they will simply start chuckling away, or worse if you have a cockerel.

Let them out and provide food and water as per their daily ration. Have a chat about the state of the weather or something that caught your eye, and have a good look around for signs of intruders, scratches at the door of the hut, the outer fence, fox spraints on the floor. Arrange the run and shade/shelter according to the weather and notice how perky the birds are. Are there any stragglers, any overtly aggressive ones, any on the nest?

Pretty much they can be left alone to their daily routine. Make sure there is dust in the dust box (if you have one) and so on. Collect any eggs you find and have a quick look around in case there are any outside.

In the evening you do almost the reverse. At the risk of preaching, I feel that you should do everything in your power to discourage rats. In an urban situation this means leaving no food about at all, so bring it in at night time, but make sure there is water in the hut overnight. If you use a hopper feeder, pick up any bits of food that might have fallen out of the side. I use a tray to collect any mess. If you feed inside the hut make sure there is no food left behind.

I use strong smelling pine sawdust on the floor of the hut, partly to disguise the aroma of chickens to the wild world of night time predators. Incidentally, around my chicken run are planted onions and garlic to achieve exactly the same job.

When the birds have started to settle themselves down for the night, usually around dusk, make sure the pop hole (door to the hut) is secure and that your security is set in place.

If the weather is frosty I give them a late afternoon feed of hard corn which keeps them warm through the night. Also add a little glycerine to the water to stop it freezing.

JOBS FOR EVERY COUPLE OF DAYS

Spend a little time handling and talking to your birds. Hold feed on your hand from time to time and get them used to you. Clean out the water dish or dispenser with soapy water and replenish it. Replenish hoppers or dishes with feed and check the grit tray.

Check the ground is not too wet and if there's grass, give it a spiking with a garden fork to increase drainage. Puddles need to be dealt with by either putting a board over, filling in with large pebbles or draining. Don't let chickens drink muddy water because it could increase the chances of them getting parasites.

Watch the birds to see if they are scratching a lot, check their legs to see if they are scaly and hold the bird, checking for mites at the vent, neck and the 'armpits'.

Check inside the hut to see how soiled the perches are. Check the perches for red mite. Have a quick look at the nesting area.

WEEKLY JOBS

In the urban situation it is important the chickens do not overtly smell and are seen to be looked after perfectly. In the country, deep littering is a normal activity. This is where the litter is covered with fresh straw, so that over the winter a layer builds up of rotting straw covered by new straw. In the spring the whole lot is removed and composted, usually by growing mushrooms on it.

With a small hut in an urban situation, this is neither feasible nor advisable. Neighbours would take umbrage as the bedding began to smell and the rats began to make small communities around the hut. Try your utmost to change the bedding weekly and clean out the hut at the same time. This is not such an onerous job with modern hen huts.

Check for evidence of intrusion. Are there any unusual holes in the hut? Can you see any gnaw marks and other scratchings? Can you see blood anywhere? Are there any eggs, or worse, eggshell?

Note: Always wear stout gloves when cleaning out the hut.

MONTHLY JOBS

You should worm your hens monthly by adding a preparation to the food or water. There are many you can buy and they change their names every couple of years, but are readily available from poultry suppliers.

Make sure the structure of the hut remains adequate, repairing any rotting wood, treating it and ensuring the structure is both waterproof and dry. Are there any parts of the house that might be a home for mites and parasites? Check under the hut and any blind spots for evidence of rats.

Treat the birds for mites and lice even if you haven't seen any.

Keep your eyes open around the feed store for evidence of any unwelcome guests.

Once a month, during your cleaning routine, disinfect the surfaces if you can.

BIMONTHLY JOBS

If you have room, move the hut and run to new soil. This doesn't have to be far from the original place; just move it on a little, enough to have fresh, non-contaminated soil beneath.

When you have done this, make sure your security precautions are changed accordingly. If you have a run with a wire skirt, make sure it is correctly buried so dogs, cats and foxes cannot get in.

If you have a fixed site for your run, perhaps filled with bark chippings, shovel the material out and compost it, replacing with new material. Wear gloves for this and make sure all of the material is removed. This ensures that the parasites that may be in the material are completely removed from the hen's reach.

SIX MONTHLY JOBS

You will need, after a year at least, to start to think about replacing your birds, and how you might integrate new birds with your existing flock. This might include visiting other poultry keepers or even joining your local poultry club. There is always something new to learn.

As the winter appears you might wish to increase the amount of litter in the hut and perhaps move it to a more sheltered position.

Check the wings of the birds and if they have been replaced in the moult since the last time they were clipped, cut the feathers on only one wing.

CHAPTER 6
CHICKEN DISEASES

Birds get sick just like people. If seems, however, that birds can get sicker than people and they can be rather hit and miss in the way they recover. There are also few places to go to get them well again. Unfortunately, if you take a chicken to a vet you are likely to get an indifferent response. It is worth hunting down a vet that specialises in chickens rather than simply popping along to your local cat and dog surgery.

Needless to say, a good hen vet is as rare as hen's teeth, so once you find the right vet, lock him or her up in a cupboard so they can't get away. The law states that it is illegal to withhold reasonable treatment from a sick animal, which basically means that if your attempts at treatment do not work within a short timeframe, you are bound to take the animal to the vet. You mustn't try one remedy after another while the animal suffers.

Just because 'Old Fred' down the road treated his birds in one way does not mean it will work with your birds at all. You must find a decent vet if your first attempts do not work, or else cull the animal in a humane way.

Most of this chapter is about good husbandry of animals. You prevent problems by allowing birds plenty of good food, good water, a clean and hygienic place to sleep and freedom from stress. That being the case there are other things we need to be on the lookout for such as mites and parasites. These will always come regardless of the regime, and you have to be on your mettle to keep your animals healthy.

I'd like to get a bit philosophical here and chat a little about husbandry, the word that is. It comes from a time in the Middle Ages when ordinary folk were completely self-sufficient. They were, to all intents, married to their land and their livestock, and from this 'relationship with land and livestock' they drew their living. It is through this labour of love that their livestock lived well. It is this idea, I believe, that any urban farmer needs to cultivate.

Poultry diseases come in all the wondrous forms we humans suffer from. There are simple infections of bacteria and viruses that we can usually inoculate the birds against. There are morphological problems of deformations and genetic disorders for which the birds are usually culled at infancy. There are parasitic problems which are uppermost in the mind of the poultry keeper and there are social problems such as feather pecking and bullying.

Hens are tenacious birds and cling on to life where they can. But the impact of age and disease often makes them simply give up the desire for life, and it is a kindness to be able to cull birds. If you are going to keep animals at all you have to have an understanding of death and be not afraid of the critical moment. If you cannot bring yourself to kill a bird humanely, find someone skilled in the matter and get them to do it, or else take the animal to the vet and pay for the job. Doing nothing when a bird is suffering is not an option.

WHAT DOES A HEALTHY BIRD LOOK LIKE?

Before you can understand what a poorly bird looks like, it is a good idea to consider what a healthy one does, how she behaves, how she eats and how her feathers look. Hens are tidy birds. They spend a great deal of time preening themselves and making sure their feathers are well oiled. In doing this they are effectively rearranging their clothing, so the wind doesn't get in. You will notice birds almost invariably face into the wind.

Birds have a bright eye and an even coloured comb. Combs and wattles that are blotchy can be a sign of trouble elsewhere, most commonly of heart and circulation problems. But a blackish spot on the comb can just be dried blood, so give it a wipe before jumping to conclusions.

Their nostrils and eyes should be dry with no redness and the hens should make warm sounding noises. You shouldn't be able to hear them breathing.

Hens are always on the lookout for things to eat or pick up. They are alert and look vitally alive. They will eat 120 g (4 oz) of food a day, plus titbits, and have an even bigger capacity for water. They may scratch once or twice, but not frequently and not in the same spot. Their legs should be clear and without blemish. They should approach the food bin with alertness, not being afraid to eat or of being attacked. They do not stay in the same place for long and when they do scratch the soil they have a rhythm to the movements and an almost happy expression.

EXTERNAL SIGNS

If your birds are under stress they will probably show it by having an unkempt look, missing feathers and a light comb. There might be blood on her if she is fighting or being bullied. If the hen is picked on by children or bothered by pets she might also look stressed. She might also be receiving too much attention from an over amorous cockerel, and you might find pecking on her saddle is making her sore.

COMPACTED CROP

Any system where an animal has to eat stones in order to grind its food has to be subject to problems! The crop is the first place where food is smashed into a pulp and this can get all blocked up. In particular, this problem occurs if the birds have access to long grass as the individual blades become tangled and when severe the material cannot pass into the stomach.

The best way to prevent this is to keep your hens on short grass. A similar problem can occur if they have too much leafy material. However, if you suspect there is a problem, you have to deal with it.

The first thing is to regularly feel the crop and if it is hard and compacted a second check a couple of hours later will confirm the problem. Use an eye dropper to pour some warm water into the beak and make the bird drink and then gently massage the crop. You might even have to turn the bird upside down and expel some of the material through the mouth.

This procedure sounds daunting for the new poultry keeper, and you are probably best having someone show you how to do it so you might gain confidence.

POULTRY PARASITES

There was a chap who sat at the entrance to his poultry cage on my allotment with whom I used to speak every morning. Unfortunately he was not a well man and I was dismayed to find he had been evicted from the allotments for a reason I was later to understand. I was offered his hen run, and on inspection I was completely amazed. There were dead bodies everywhere, rotting carcasses and skeletons, and a complete mess in the hen house. Food was spilled along the floor of the hut and rats had tunnelled themselves an underground city. It took a long time to sort out, I can tell you. But then whenever the hens got sick it was hard not to blame the previous owner. Eventually I dug out all the soil and carted it to my allotment where no birds could reach and replaced it with a system where I could remove the substrate and compost it. I eventually chose bark chippings which, although they took a long time to compost, kept their shape and didn't go mushy in the rain.

Poultry parasites appear from nowhere. They come from feed, from wild birds, from the hens themselves and even if you have new birds on virgin soil you will find that at some point you will experience poultry parasites.

Poultry louse

When the chicken dusts itself in soil and shakes itself down, it is actually trying to keep populations of poultry lice down. This yellowish, flat louse is found at the hen's bottom and neck, where the bird is warmest. They lay their eggs at the base of feathers and as they hatch they make the bird scratch. The poultry louse is not an enormous burden on the bird but it does irritate them. Birds with other problems are made worse for poultry lice infestation. The louse lives by scratching away at the skin of the bird and eating it, which is pretty horrid, but we all have to live.

Badly infested birds lose weight and egg production is diminished. You get patches of skin showing where the bird has scratched itself and this in turn can lead to bullying and feather pecking.

Depluming mite

This animal does what its name suggests. It annoys the birds so much that the bird pulls its feathers out. The depluming mite is a summertime pest and lays eggs as the winter begins, the bird gets some freedom only to find they're back the following May.

Scaly leg mite

The beautiful scales on the legs of chickens can be home to a mite that causes them to deform. The same mite affects the wattles and combs too. The legs become swollen and the scales puffed out so the whole leg looks like a scab. The mite burrows under the slow growing, raised, crusty scales and drives the birds mad with irritation. This is very unpleasant for the bird and it can go lame after a while.

One treatment for this is to immerse the leg in alcohol. I have used meths but surgical spirit is better because it isn't poisonous.

Mites and lice can be dealt with by a monthly dusting of powder. If your flock is very small, two or three hens, you can get away with a six weekly regime. You can buy the insecticide in powder or spray form; they both work in the same way. Wear gloves, goggles and a mask. Hold the bird so it cannot struggle and rub in the powder, reaching inside the feathers, in the bottom, around the wings and in the neck. When you buy the treatment make sure you read the instructions carefully and also take account of any withdrawal period for eating eggs and flesh.

If you do not regularly clear these pests you will find that numbers build up very rapidly. Within days of infestation taking place the mite population can increase to thousands, so the important thing is to be sure you are on top of the situation by constant vigilance.

Red mite and northern fowl mite

This is going to be the first poultry disease you come across, and it isn't that pretty. Everything is fine with the hens and they are laying well, until you notice there is something not quite right with the legs and the birds seem a little more irritable than before. You think nothing of it until, on changing the bedding in the house, you notice red patches on the underside of the perches. When you look even closer they consist of little spider-like creatures, all red and moving over each other. If you shine a light on them they will start to crawl slowly away from the light and you begin to realise they are red because they are full of your chicken's blood.

Red mite is the most common problem chickens face. They are spiders with eight legs and look like crabs. During the day they shelter from the sunlight by hiding in crevices and at night they crawl out like some horrid plague to suck the blood from your hen's eggs. While they are on the perch the hens don't seem to be bothered by this and they behave as though there were no problems. However, when the numbers of mites increase the birds become anaemic and listless. The wounds caused by the mites become infected; the legs can become scaly and painful.

Northern fowl mites are on the birds all the time and so their affect is worse. The birds become listless, stay in one spot, scratch and are bad tempered, likely to peck out where before they were simply accepting of human company. They lose feather condition, the combs and wattles are droopy and pale and they cause the vent to bleed, causing streaks of blood on the eggs. Egg laying slows down and the flock goes into decline.

Infestations of mites can cause secondary problems such as fowl cholera and anaemia. These occur because of the lack of blood and, let's face it, a hen hasn't got much anyway. The ability of the bird to replace the blood it has lost is affected and therefore the immune system stops functioning properly.

Diagnosing northern fowl mite is not pleasant. The mites congregate where the bird is warm, and the eggs and faeces stain the feathers. If you move the feathers away you will see them and in a heavily infested bird you will find the mites run onto your hands.

TREATING RED MITE

This is an easy, though gruesome, task. Look inside the house and you will find the mites huddled together and crawling over each other. If you have a plastic hutch it is an easy job to wash them away and treat with disinfectant afterwards. Make sure you are able to remove them all, look in the nest box and any cranny you can find. If you have a wooden hut, turn the blowlamp on them and then treat with mite powder and plug up any crannies with putty. A garden jet is also a good idea, and again, don't forget the nest box and everywhere the birds will congregate. There is no point treating the birds alone if you are not going to treat the hut.

It is important that wooden houses are well maintained as they age. You will be offering hiding spaces for mites if the woodwork is rotting and the structure has become a bit wobbly.

You can also dust the chicken's legs with mite powder or spray, perhaps something based on pyrethroids. There are quite a number of powders and sprays; one I have used often is a citrus oil that stays on the legs for some time offering some continued protection.

TREATING NORTHERN FOWL MITE

For northern fowl mite it is essential to apply approved insecticides to the affected birds. If you do not use insecticides on the hens you can get a number of organic treatments that do not work so well, but are effective enough if you keep to the minimum periods for re-treatment. In this case you are more managing your flock rather than keeping them completely free from mites.

If you are introducing new hens to an existing flock, especially if they are battery hens, do so gradually and make sure the newcomers are properly treated. A sudden influx of mites can cause a hen considerable harm.

Keeping mite numbers down to a minimum is important and you should allow the birds to do it their way too. Dust areas are an essential way the bird keeps external parasites down. You can improve the effectiveness if you add some finely graded wood ash to the dusting areas.

INTERNAL PARASITES

The hen's gut is a simple affair and can be home to a number of highly specialised creatures able to eke out a decent living inside the bird. You rarely get parasites in the stomach of the bird because of its fairly harsh chemical environment, but the crop and the intestines can be badly infected.

Internal parasites are frequently referred to as worms, but this isn't really helpful if you want to understand the different types of organisms infecting your birds. There is a fundamental relationship between the bird, its parasites and the soil they are living on. The birds ingest various animals when they are foraging and these are frequently infected themselves with parasites whose real target is the chicken. As the parasite lives in the bird it reproduces and its young or eggs fall out of the hen onto the soil in its poo. This will then infect the soil and any other insects in the soil and thence pass back into another hen. If hens are allowed to stay only on the same land for a long period the amount of parasites will build up in the soil, making it certain that new poultry will become infected.

For this reason it is customary to move your hens around so they cannot cause such a build up. Bare land can take six months to be free of parasites, and longer in some rare cases. So if you are running your birds on grass you need at least five different places to put the run on, so you can move them around the garden and allow an appropriate amount of time for any parasite build up to go away. When hens get onto fresh pasture they perk up and regain vigour for life. You can see the urgency with which they run to new grass and new earth to scratch away at it.

In the town you might not have enough space for a lot of changes of position. In this case semi free ranging on some other substrate is important. If this is the case, keep your birds in a run where you can remove the basic material (I use bark) and compost it. This way you remove the eggs and larvae of intestinal parasites at source and it is easier to keep your hens free of problems.

Roundworms

These are at least as long as your finger, though not as fat. They live in the large intestine and produce larvae that bury themselves into the wall of the intestine. They cause the bird to lose weight, but are generally not a threat to the animal, except who wants to feed worms?

Hairworms

These are thin and about a centimetre long. They can cause considerable damage to the guts and the eggs infect earthworms and then are passed back to the hens when eaten. They are difficult to remove from affected birds and you should always change the ground they are on.

Gapeworms

These are found in the lungs of the bird and cause respiratory problems from a rasping breath to ultimate death. They are most common in young birds. Again the infection comes via earthworms, so you need to be certain the flooring soil is not affected in any way, probably best by keeping them on bark in an urban situation. Other animals, such as common beetles, also carry this worm.

Tapeworms

These are not normally any problem for hens, but they need treating none the less. You might not know your hen has a tapeworm at all, but the general purpose worming preparations deal with them effectively. There are large tapeworms that stay in one segment or fall apart, infecting the ground in faeces. The small tapeworms can even block up the duodenum.

Treatment

A number of things can have an adverse affect on poultry health and immunity. It sometimes takes a variety of problems to make a bird sick, frequently affecting their ability to cope with intestinal parasites so it really is important to keep parasites under control. They are usually treated by adding chemicals to feed. For most purposes, there is a solution called flubenvet. Over the years, as strains of worms become immune to the chemicals we use against them, there will be new products on the market. Go to the vets or agricultural suppliers and buy the appropriate wormer.

Most wormers are simply added to the feed where the powder sticks to the pellets and the hens do not have any problems taking it. Some are added to water, but not many.

Always make sure you treat the birds exactly as the instructions on the packet indicate. Also make sure you comply with any withdrawal periods for not eating eggs after treatment.

Don't get confused

There are lots of preparations out there that look like wormers but actually are not. They are possibly useful in keeping your hen in good order and have a beneficial affect on their general health, immunity and their ability to fight worm infection. But they are not specifically wormers. I have not used natural remedies for worming birds, usually strong garlic preparations, because I don't fancy the idea of garlic flavoured eggs.

MAREK'S DISEASE

Jozsef Marek first described this condition in 1907, though he had no way of knowing what the cause was. In fact it is a viral infection of chickens of the herpes type. In the last hundred years various mutations have appeared throughout the USA and Europe, particularly in response to broiler production of hens in sheds.

The major route of infection is from dust in broiler units, or large free-range sheds which are in fact not free range at all. The disease comes first from the lungs and continues to affect the whole of the bird. A small flock of birds in the garden is unlikely to get this disease, unless you have bought rescue hens from a farmer. It is also thought that there is a transport route for this virus via some insects, though the actual means of transmission is not clear.

It is known that vertical transmission does not occur, so eggs are hatched virus free and this gives a plausible way out for the home poultry keeper. The virus does survive well out of the bird and has been known to be resistant to certain disinfectants. Keeping young birds away from older ones is an important step.

Symptoms

The first noticeable affect of this disease is that the hen's eyes become lumpy and the iris granular in appearance. Then the bird begins to become paralysed and unable to walk. Firstly the legs go stiff, then the wings and finally the neck. At the same time the bird loses weight and finally goes blind. The feathers are lost in some cases and the skin looks all lumpy.

Birds also suffer from 'floppy broiler syndrome' that is caused by tumors in the central nervous system. Then tumors occur internally in the major organs.

Clearly, when under extreme physical stress from Marek's disease, birds often succumb to other diseases.

Treatment and prevention

There is no known treatment for Marek's disease although chicks from large commercial hatcheries are routinely vaccinated with a number of serums. There are increasing numbers of suppliers who vaccinate for the disease in the egg, probably for commercial reasons.

Genetic selection for a gene that infers some natural resistance to the virus was under way with the cross-breeding of White Leghorns, which have a large measure of immunity, with other breeds. However, the use of serum immunisation has put this research on the back boiler for economic reasons.

Prevention is further improved by the way we keep hens. Commercial keepers use a combination of excellent hygiene and an all in – all out system of farming. If you introduce new birds to a large number of old ones you are more likely to pass on the disease. Similarly, hen material left behind in the hut will be contagious, and therefore sheds need to be completely cleaned and disinfected before new stock arrives.

I said earlier that insects could act as reservoirs for infection. Making an environment that is not conducive to insects is not an easy task, but certainly a clean, well mucked out shed and run is an important and helpful factor for the home keeper.

If you are interested in rearing young chicks they should be kept away from older birds for the longest period, possibly 16 weeks. This allows them to develop their immune system to its fullest extent before being exposed to possibly infected material.

Finally, some reports have shown that the provision of plenty of calcium in the diet, crushed shell and the like, helps the young bird to develop a strong immune system, and this might help in the fight against many diseases as well as Marek's disease.

COCCIDIOSIS

Coccidiosis is probably the worst problem the home poultry keeper faces. It is very common and painful. It is also very costly in commercial flocks.

Coccidia occur everywhere in the environment, particularly in the soil, water, the guts of most animals, and certainly in droppings. They can be found on surfaces and even in the air. They are protozoan, single-celled creatures that spend most of their time enclosed in a cyst, waiting for the right conditions to come along for the next stage of their life cycle. It is almost guaranteed that your poultry will come into contact with coccidia at some point in their lives, if not daily. Infection mostly comes from the ingestion of material that once had faeces on or near it. If you have other pets, be careful where they poo.

The cyst forms of coccidia are very resistant to all kinds of environmental factors. You can disinfect them and they will still survive. In some cases they can be boiled or frozen, dried or blasted with chemicals and they will continue to live. Out of all the many thousand types of coccidia, only seven of them infect poultry and most birds can cope happily with some forms of the infection. The symptoms will vary according to how many coccidia are in the gut of the bird and how well the bird copes with other infections.

The bird will suffer from coccidiosis to varying degrees depending on the number of coccidia they are infected with and factors as seemingly trivial as the weather. Birds will appear to get well and then take a step backward for reasons you will not be able to pinpoint. The symptoms come on very quickly and you should always keep your eyes on your birds so you can spot exactly when they are 'off colour'. Some instances of dosing with vitamins, particularly cod-liver oil, have produced excellent results.

If you have rescue hens that are now free ranging and eating a lot of wild food, the chances are they will fall prey to the disease more easily than you would expect. Despite appearances, ex-battery hens are usually completely free from internal parasites and when they get them it can be quite a shock to the system.

Coccidia life cycle

Coccidia have a trick that keeps them on top of the game when it comes to treatment. They have a sexual and non sexual side to their life cycle. In the bird's intestine the coccidial cells reproduce sexually. Mutations that occur in this process, which sometimes help the parasite to fight our attempts to control them, create offspring that are sometimes stronger or more virulent than before. These are passed out of the body of the hen to be ingested by another. The new coccidia then reproduce non sexually to produce millions of new organisms in the hen's gut.

Symptoms

The coccidia push themselves into the lining of the gut, which irritates the birds, causes runny poo and can kill in some circumstances. This makes them feel generally unwell and on top of this the gut is not working at the optimum rate. It causes the bird to set into malnutrition, and you will see blood in very runny droppings.

The main visible signs apart from this are lethargy and loss of condition. The birds lose weight and muscles become weak and floppy. Once this happens the immune system is unable to cope with other infections and the bird is on a downward spiral towards serious ill health.

At this stage the birds fall prey to other problems, general infections and parasitic attack. They look listless, their combs become very pale and floppy, and they are likely to be bullied. Badly affected birds look near to death, scruffy, with closed eyes and dropping wings. Sometimes the shock of the infection can lead to the sudden death of the bird.

One of the major associated diseases afflicting birds with coccidiosis is necrotic enteritis, which is caused by the common bacterium clostridium perfringens. This organism is even more common than coccidia and normally causes no problems in poultry. But combined with coccidiosis, the birds are unable to cope with the new infection. The growth of the bacterium releases toxic substances in the gut and if it is already damaged by coccidia the bird will succumb.

Managing the disease

Good management of the hens and their runs is an important part of keeping them disease free. Try to maintain as dry conditions as you can, which forces the coccidia into the cyst stage. It can then be easily removed from the top soil at least by simple digging and replacing with fresh soil. Make sure the house is well ventilated but without cold winds and that there are no wet areas inside. Try not to keep the birds' water inside the hen house.

Avoid keeping too many hens in the run. A small hut is big enough for only two hens, and a good 5 m² is needed for each bird. Lots of birds pooing in the run is asking for trouble. Try to put boards over the run so the birds do not simply peck at the soil.

Not a battery hen disease

Birds kept in battery conditions have been relatively free from the problem because of the requirement for very high bio-security. For this reason, as described earlier, rescue birds can suddenly fall prey to the problem. However, the increasing number of free-range and organic birds being kept has led to an inevitable increase in coccidiosis because of the greater number of birds scratching in infected soil.

Treatment

The lack of an easily applied and completely effective vaccine means that other chemical treatments are required, especially for the home poultry keeper. There are a number on the market, and your vet can suggest the one you should use. Normally put in drinking water, they provide a good measure of control that keeps numbers of parasites at bay.

There are two classes of drugs. Coccidiostats arrest or inhibit the growth of intracellular parasites. But this type of drug can make the bird more sensitive to coccidia in the future. They work by making complex chemicals on the cell surface of the parasite. The other chemicals are called coccidiocidals, which destroy coccidia during their development inside the gut. If you suspect coccidiosis then have a chat with your vet and take the appropriate steps straight away.

MYCOPLASMA

The word *myco*plasma initially makes the biologist think of fungi as mycology is the study of mushrooms and fungi. However the *plasma* part of the term is often used to refer to protozoan animals. The truth is that the genus mycoplasma is actually a bacterium without much of a cell wall, consequently the confusion about what it actually is. There are over 100 species of this genus and most of them cause no problem in the hen (or humans for that matter).

However, in certain circumstances the bacterium can cause clinical symptoms. These range from sneezing to heavy breathing. The air sacs become infected and the bird will then become listless, lose weight and breathe heavily. For all intents it looks as though the animal has a bad dose of the flu. Note: this is not avian flu (the bird would be dead by now).

You can treat this with antibiotics, but you must make sure you contact the vet if you believe there is an outbreak.

PECKING BIRDS AND CANNIBALISM

The biggest shock new poultry keepers have is when they realise that hens are not like any other animal we come across. They are often ruthless in their desire to be at the top of the pecking order, they will delight in the taste of blood, will peck at their young and fight for eggs if one is ever cracked. Perhaps they are like humans after all!

I once had the misfortune of a broody coop break and the chicks got out among the other ladies. They were very quickly severely attacked by the ladies, though not the cockerel, a formidable creature, who was gentleness itself with the youngsters.

The interesting point is that hens are often harsh, difficult, bad tempered with each other – though they're not humans. Not the kind of girls you would like to get to know.

Pecking

All birds peck at each other. It is a function of being a game bird. Don't forget that this impulse is so strong that for many thousands of years humans have used them for entertainment in the fighting ring – thankfully now illegal. And of course the term 'pecking order' is firmly established in language. By their very nature hens peck at each other. Males compete violently for females and hens compete for food and sometimes nesting space. There is also competition for roosting room.

All of this is quite normal, but there sometimes comes a point when the occasional skirmish becomes habitual pecking and some birds can find themselves under severe attack all day long. When this occurs the end result, if not dealt with, is the death of the bird followed by cannibalism. Just how and why these birds, which for so long are as good as gold, suddenly become cannibalistic bullies is not clear.

What are the signs?

You will see birds pecking or feather pulling and it is usually the same birds that are the victims. When enough feathers have been removed, the skin is attacked to draw blood, at which point more birds become interested. Normal 'pecking order' type pecking usually affects the back and tail of birds. Aggressive, pathological pecking can be at the head and face, the wings, the vents and neck.

Once blood is drawn it is not unusual for pecking to be so frenzied that it results in the death of the victim. This unpleasant situation is certainly undesirable, but can also lead to the spread of disease around the flock.

Overcrowding

Some suspect this phenomenon begins as a result of overcrowding. This is easy to believe in broiler sheds, but less so for the backyard hen with all the space a bird ever needs.

However, there are some warning signs to look out for. The entrance to the hen house, whatever it may be, can cause a bottleneck of birds that can trigger problems. The space and height of the roosting bars can do much the same. Small arcs and small runs with only enough room for the birds to move around (although infinitely better than the conditions for caged birds) can lead to problems, especially if the hens are large.

Disease

The presence of disease or infection can trigger aggressive attacks. Scaly leg and red mite in particular can cause unwanted interest from birds. This is a function of the feeding reflex, where a bird sees an object and pecks at it to see if it is edible. Making sure your birds are free from infestation and healthy is good practice in itself, but in this case has a double importance.

If the parasite load on the land is high birds can become irritated and consequently more prone to 'pecking order' attacks, which in turn can lead to other problems. Make sure your birds are moved around, if possible onto fresh land.

Feeding and water

Competition for feed is proportionate to the number of birds you have feeding at a particular station. Where this is high, for example when not all the birds can feed easily at one time, problems can occur. This might be alleviated by changing your food type. Mash might appear to be easier to digest to humans, but takes a bird longer to eat than pellets. Adding stations for feed can be an easy way of avoiding problems. The same goes for water and places to scratch and dig up grubs.

Malnourished birds can resort to feather pulling and feather eating in order to provide the nutrients they need.

Light

Bright light can lead to problems, particularly for urban hens, as can shafts of bright light interspersed with dark areas. In my experience this sends them a bit loopy anyway. It has long been a problem in broiler sheds where the light from the roof windows creates spaces of light and dark. Homemade lights used in an attempt to keep winter birds laying can also cause problems if they are too bright or in the wrong-sized building.

Boredom

If you can make life interesting for your birds they are less likely to fight. You will have happy birds if, when you let them out of the hut in the morning, they can sprint over the coop to the hanging sprouts you have left for them, or scratch through some rotted compost to find some worms. Also helpful are well-defined and easily cleared hiding places.

Heat

High temperatures can trigger the problem. In the summer try to make sure there is plenty of ventilation and that hut temperatures are as cool as possible.

AVIAN FLU

When bird flu became a real problem a few years ago in the Far East, imports of chicks into the UK were banned from any country that had the disease. This caused a huge upset, especially with keepers of rare breed poultry. In the UK we had gone through a terribly upsetting time with foot and mouth disease in cattle and pigs, and poultry keepers were worried that the government would impose the same solution: the wholesale slaughter of chickens.

Many breeds simply would not survive a wholesale cull in a single part of the country. The other proposed solution was simply locking birds up in sheds to stop droppings from migrating geese and swans landing in the way of our chickens. For most people the thought of having to do this was more than they could bear; after all, the reason for keeping hens in the first place was to be able to give them a happy, natural life.

There have been outbreaks of avian flu in the UK, perhaps most recently in the Bernard Matthews turkey factory, but none have caused any of the supposed problems for poultry keepers.

The virus causing the flu is the H5N1 strain of the flu virus. To put the worries of this disease into context, the virus that caused the 1919 pandemic was a H1N1 virus. The fear is that H5N1 will easily mutate and become infectious to humans.

But none of this means it is unsafe to keep poultry

You will not know if your birds are infected; they will simply die, and very quickly at that. This shows the importance of paying for a post-mortem to be carried out for any birds that die suddenly. In an urban situation it is unlikely in the extreme your birds will have H5N1 because for the moment the only possible route of infection is from wild birds, normally those able to migrate long distances from the Far East, notably swans.

FIGHTING DAMAGE

Birds that fight should be separated and allowed their own space for some time before trying to reintroduce them. The problem is related to a natural impulse within the bird that makes it aggressive. Males in particular will attack anything that 'pushes its button'. Biologically speaking, aggression is triggered by a sign stimulus, which might be a large comb or even a certain coloured eye. The bird's reaction to a sign stimulus is also affected by other factors, such as the amount of space and roosting space, the number of hens, or the amount of food.

Birds will damage themselves quite significantly given the chance and make each other quite sick from stress alone.

Fighting with cats and dogs

Most hens will cope with cats. The ferocity of their beak and the sharpness of their claws are sufficient to make any sensible cat attack only once. The cat will come off worse. However, when it comes to dogs the situation is quite reversed. A dog will easily kill or severely damage a hen or cockerel; a problem that is common with spaniel and terrier type dogs more than anything else.

Don't give up hope

If your hen is alive but wounded there is plenty of hope. One of the advantages of being a fundamentally simple animal is that they heal well. Bring the animal inside where it is warm and free from draughts, and away from competition from other birds or the attention of any other animals. Provide water and a little food and leave it overnight. You can stand it in a cardboard box. If the animal is going to survive the night the likelihood is that it will make a complete recovery.

This hospitalisation method, where you actually do very little, has proven enough to see many injured or sick hens brought back from the brink.

CALCIUM DEFICIENCY

You have taken everyone's advice and all is going well with your birds, but all of a sudden they peck out their feathers and become bald, especially on their bellies. You cannot stop them from scratching and they progressively get worse. They seem to have a lot of grit and have a normal ration, but for some reason they have developed a deficiency of calcium.

This is a common problem for many keepers and the simplest way to cure it is to give them a pot or two of yoghurt, which they love and which gets them back to normal – though it might take a while for the feathers to return.

FOOD SUPPLEMENTS FOR HEALTHY BIRDS

Poultry do well, like humans, when they are on good vitamins and health-giving foods. I would like to mention just three that are in general use.

Garlic

This is an amazing plant that has antifungal, antibiotic and antiviral properties. Some people crush a clove into the drinking water, but I do not like to give anything but water in case they don't like the flavour or smell. Some crush and chop garlic into the food. You can buy preparations based on garlic that are said to help regulate the numbers of internal parasites, but it is probably better to depend on accepted worming preparations for that.

Garlic will keep your flock in good health, but there is no need to give them too much because the flavour can come out in the eggs.

Apple cider vinegar

Once a week I give two tablespoons of apple cider vinegar in a day's supply of water. This adds vitamins and the health benefits are far ranging. You always get good strong feathers and bright eyes when the birds are treated and their general health seems to improve. It helps the immune system without bypassing it (as with antibiotics) and it fights bacterial infections.

Cod liver oil

This gives excellent health benefits, from healthy joints to multivitamins for general health. A weekly tablespoon dribbled over the feed is all you need and it makes for excellent perky birds. It is also good to use as a glue when adding wormer to the feed. Sprinkle the feed with cod liver oil first and then follow with the wormer. This way the powder sticks to the feed better.

CHICKEN DISEASES AT A GLANCE

Disease	Symptom	Treatment	Likely outcome
Aspergillosis	Fungal infection causing respiratory problems. Can be found in broodies breathing in the fungal spores. They breathe heavily and in adults the combs go blue	Increase ventilation to control infection. Change the bedding	Animals rarely die, and slowly recover
Avian influenza (Bird flu) Not likely at all	Mild form: listlessness, do not eat, cannot breathe, diarrhoea, dramatic drop in number of eggs. Worst cases: wattles and comb go blue, bloody nasal discharge, black (dark red) spots appear on comb, legs and wattles, the hen dies	None. Seek advice straight away. The authorities will have to be involved	The flock will be destroyed
Bronchitis	Coughing, nasal discharge, wheezing, low egg production, runny eggs	None available. The older the bird, the worse it gets	They will recover, but the virus remains in the body
Coccidiosis	Lethargy, loss of condition, loss of weight, muscles become weak and floppy. They look listless, combs become very pale and floppy. Badly affected birds look near to death, scruffy, closed eyes, drooping wings	Coccidiostats arrest or inhibit the growth of intracellular parasites. Coccidiocidals destroy coccidia during their development inside the gut. Clean regime is important	They should recover, but untreated they will die
Egg drop syndrome	Birds look healthy. Eggs have thin or no shells. Numbers of eggs reduce dramatically	None, but the second string of eggs are usually unaffected	

119

Disease	Symptom	Treatment	Likely outcome
Fowl cholera Not that common	Dead birds. Fever, low food intake, nasal discharge, untidy feathers, diarrhoea	Urban pigeons and rats have this – keep them apart from your hens. Vaccination is available. Sulphonomides can treat symptoms – garlic is full of sulphonamides, but you need veterinary help	Likely the birds will die
Fowl pox Not likely to be a problem	Cuts appear which scab over	None, but vaccination available	Reduced laying and growth. Birds do recover
Marek's disease	Lumpy eyes, paralysis	None, but vaccination available for chicks	Best to cull the animal
Mycoplasmosis	Sneezing to heavy breathing. Air sacs become infected and the bird will then become listless, lose weight and breathe heavily. Sticky discharge from the nostrils	Antibiotics available	Birds rarely die if treated
Necrotic enteritis	The original gut rot. Dark, blood-stained diarrhoea, wasting birds	Antibiotics available	Birds should recover, but will never be in top health
Newcastle disease Not likely to be a problem	Sore throat, hoarse, swollen head, runny nasal discharge, gasping for breath	None, but vaccination available	Animal can die in certain cases. Seek advice. Humans get conjunctivitis from same virus
Viral arthritis Not likely to occur	Swelling joints, lameness, stiff tendons. Can affect the intestinal tract	None	Best to cull the animal

CHAPTER 7

CHICKS – MAKING YOUR OWN

When you have kept hens for some time the question almost invariably arises: 'Shall I have a go at raising chicks?' The idea of fluffy new hens is captivating and soon enough you will be thinking seriously of getting a cockerel, or failing that an incubator and buying some fertilised eggs.

WHY FERTILISED EGGS?

In order to get fertilised hens' eggs you need to have a cockerel – that part should be obvious. What is less obvious is that he has to be up to the job, so to speak, and this takes some time. As hens come into point of lay at somewhere around 20 weeks, so cockerels come into their maturity. But they are not so mature as to successfully produce enough sperm for a party of hens, and this means having him around for quite some time. The fact that he is noisy might mean he is unwelcome in an urban situation.

If you use a broody hen to sit on eggs you will have to have a separate coop for her and her offspring once they have hatched, which will mean more space that you might not have available. Although it takes 21 days for the eggs to hatch once they are incubated, she might be collecting her clutch for five or so days too, so the whole process will take the best part of a month.

For these reasons it is probably better if you go down the incubator and bought eggs route in a truly urban situation.

WHEN A HEN GOES BROODY

Hormonal changes in the hen stop her from laying eggs and she decides to sit. She will sit in one place all the time, going out only once a day to eat, drink and poo. She will start to cluck if you go near her and even peck at you.

The broody hen has stopped laying but has in her nest a number of eggs that she has collected or simply protected. You can put fertile eggs underneath her from other nest boxes and she will care for them, turning them around and keeping them warm. The turning is an important part of the process because not only do they need heat, the membranes inside the egg must not stick to the shell. If this happens the egg will not develop.

She will accept other eggs – bantams', ducks' and geese eggs – and incubate them all, but she may not look after them once they have hatched.

Fertilised eggs remain viable for around two weeks if the temperature is not too cold. A broody hen will start to sit when there are a few eggs together, and she can look after around ten to a dozen or so. Once the temperature reaches blood heat, or pretty near, the eggs will begin to develop as though they were all laid on the same day. Consequently the batch of chicks will emerge on more or less the same day.

The broody hen will lose feathers from her underside so the eggs can benefit from the heat of her skin without insulation. She will also start deep clucking, a repetitive cluck that is quite different to the norm.

STOPPING A HEN FROM GOING BROODY

Hybrid hens do not go broody very well, and if they do (more likely in the second and third year) they are not very consistent during the process. If the eggs go cold they will die. If you do not want a hen to go broody she must be removed to her own area, fairly confined and away from her nesting box. It will take anything up to two weeks to get her back to normal. If this fails, keeping her on a mesh floor with plenty of ventilation does the trick – a bit of cold wind is enough to put anyone off laying eggs!

WHAT YOU NEED FOR A HEN TO INCUBATE HER EGGS

Obviously you need a broody hen. You can stimulate broodiness by putting pot eggs (golf balls work well and I have even used paperweights) in the nest and, if you have the right breed (Silkies are best), a hen will start to brood. The process is going to be a long one for the animal (try sitting more or less in the same position for a month!) so make her as comfortable as you can by treating her for lice and worming her beforehand.

You need a broody box, which is essentially a hutch with a nest area and a built-in run for the chicks. Then you will need some way of feeding and watering. It is a good idea if this can be managed away from the nest area and watch her so that you can be sure she has 'done all three' which should not take more than 20 minutes. Try to remove her poo because it smells very strongly and can attract predators. She should have access to water all the time, and a small amount of feed nearby. She will also still need grit.

She will not be interested in scraps or any of the other normal hen activities; her whole metabolism is changed to hatch her eggs.

You will need to site the broody box well out of the way of the other hens so there are no attentions from other birds.

Humidity

My first hens were hatched in an old garden shed and they were not that successful, half of them not making it at all. I learned this was due to humidity when I bought a broody coop where the nesting area had no floor at all. Moisture from the earth is an important part of the incubating process. Water has to be added, gently, when the hen is away from the nest. A teaspoon sprinkled every couple of days will suffice, so long as the water is warm.

HATCHING

It takes 21 days from the onset of incubation to hatching, so keep a calendar. You might be a day out, so don't panic. You will begin to hear piping from within the eggs, behaviour designed to bring the chicks to hatching stage so there is one brood all hatched within hours of each other.

The hen will need to be removed from the chicks as normal for a break, but be very careful when lifting her. While the hen is away make sure the broken shell is removed, but try not to help the birds escape the shell. You will have to keep an eye on their progress without causing too much fuss and cooling the chicks too much. After a few hours the majority of the eggs will have been hatched. Avoid handling the stragglers and when it becomes obvious that any eggs are not going to hatch, dispose of them.

Leave the chicks to fluff out, which will not take too long. Their reserves from the egg will last them for at least three days, so don't be worried if they are not eating.

Keep them together in the broody hut run with mum until they are at least a week old. Provide chick crumbs and a light bedding – I use sawdust. It doesn't have to be too deep, a couple of centimetres, no more than four at the most. During the first couple of days of life they are fine on a few sheets of newspaper, but after no more than three days into their life, get some bedding down. I use a wooden board to chaperone the chicks to mum while I work in the coop.

The hen will soon start to teach the chicks how to eat. Mum will provide all the heat the chicks need and the only other thing they need is water. There are umpteen stories of chicks drowning in water – make sure you use a good quality chick waterer. I like to provide them cool boiled water, but this isn't completely necessary.

Each evening both hen and chicks will be shut in and you will have the same regime as for the adult hens for a while. Above all, keep the chicks dry and free from wind and draughts as far as possible. This is why a shed makes an excellent broody coop because they can have the run of the floor.

The chicks will grow rapidly over the next few weeks. At three weeks they will have to be in their own run, with mother, so they have ample room for running around. Then you have the dreaded decision of what to do with the cockerels.

SEXING CHICKS

The problem is that half of your brood are going to be males and we have already discussed the urban situation being best without all those cockerels crowing so very early in the morning. So you need to be aware and have a plan in mind. Maybe you live in a place where the noise doesn't matter. Perhaps you have friends or fellow poultry lovers who will take them off your hands, or you have produced a rare breed chicken for which there is a ready market.

On the other hand you might just hate your neighbours and revel in waking them up. It's up to you, but if you decide to dispatch them you will have to work out which are males. You do not have the pressure of commercial breeders who have to remove the males as soon as they are hatched because they do not wish to waste valuable feed on an animal that will produce nothing. Wait until the male characteristics – the larger comb, tail feathers and more upright stance – appear. Then it is easier to dispatch them by neck dislocation. Killing a chick is no easy task on the emotions, so wait.

INCUBATION BY MACHINE

There are dozens of incubators on the market, some expensive, automatic and fairly fool proof, others cheap and requiring you to do everything yourself. Do not choose a machine on price alone. For a start they come in different sizes, holding varying numbers of eggs. I would suggest that the smaller one is suitable for the urban situation, but only you know how many hens you can keep.

There are basically four types of machine: still air, with or without automatic rotation, and fan assisted, with or without automatic rotation.

Still air incubators

Basically this is a box with a bulb in it. Some of the older ones control the temperature by moving the bulb; others have a thermostat switching the light on and off. They sometimes come with automatic egg turning systems, but rarely. These machines are budget priced and frankly the results can be hit and miss until you get used to operating them.

Fan-assisted incubators

More expensive, they give better results. Temperature and humidity are more constantly controlled and the mechanisms for moving eggs are usually better made.

Moving the eggs

In the nest the broody hen will move the eggs around at frequent intervals. This ensures that the whole embryo is uniformly warm. But there is a more important reason for turning eggs. The weight of the embryo in the egg settles down and this can cause the membranes to stick to the shell resulting in deformities in the developing chick. To prevent such damage the egg must be turned, otherwise it will not develop.

If you are turning by hand, try to do so at intervals no longer than six hours. Normally the egg will be fine all night while you are asleep, but make sure you do not leave it the same way up every night. This is achieved by marking the shell with a dot and turning the egg an odd number of times each day. If you turn it an even number the shell will always be the same way up each night.

Try to have a five-turn regime, turning the eggs by 180 degrees each time. This will mean that you have dots up one night and dots down the next. Eggs need to be turned in this manner until two or three days before they are due to hatch, by which time there are no real membranes to damage because they are all covered with feathers!

An automatic egg-moving mechanism does the whole job by machine. However I don't trust them to work continually – things break don't they? So I instigate the same routine of five checks each day just to be sure the whole thing is working and then I am satisfied that all is well. If the machine were to break and I had not bothered to check for 24 hours, then disaster might well ensue.

Where to put the incubator

For a start, there is no place for such equipment in a busy room where people, pets and children are coming in and out. The room should be quiet and unused, with no extra heating. The incubator should be placed on a stable table where it is not in danger of being knocked off or moved around harshly. You should ensure there is a constant flow of air around the incubator and you have everything you need to hand. The incubator should not be in direct sunlight or near any other forms of heat.

Cleaning the incubator

Before you put your eggs in the machine, make sure everything is clean and disinfected. Avoid smells and use only a diluted solution of Milton or its equivalent. Leave the incubator open to the air until dried so that any aromas can disperse.

How to buy fertilised eggs

There are plenty of sellers of fertilised eggs on the internet, but getting them through the post can be quite hazardous. They have to be kept at a temperature between 5 and 10°C (41 and 50°F). Eggs should be stored point down and should be no older than seven days.

If this is your first attempt at hatching eggs you are probably best to find a local supplier of the breed you want to hatch. Your local poultry club or the breed society will have all the contacts you need. Then at least you can be sure of few transport problems and you will get some much welcome advice. You cannot get enough advice because this will improve your confidence. Much of this is about confidence.

Temperature

Temperature is the most important factor in successful incubation. Before you actually start, test the equipment by putting some warm water in the humidity tray and set the temperature. The temperature should be or 37.7°C (100°F). The unit should maintain this temperature for at least 24 hours before you continue. Like cheese making, the temperature should be as exact as you can get it; a fluctuation of a single degree will substantially alter the performance of the eggs.

Humidity

The amount of water in the air is also an important part of the hatching process. For most of the time the humidity should be around 50%. A couple of days before hatching the humidity should be increased a little to around 60%. Humidity is controlled in two ways: by adding water to the humidity tray and manipulating air vents on the lid of the unit. In more expensive units you will find a digital readout of temperature and humidity, but with the cheaper versions it is either guessed or worked out.

GUESSING THE HUMIDITY

As long as there is water in the pan (always add warm water so the temperature doesn't fluctuate too much), there will be moisture in the air, and humidity isn't so critical at this stage. A couple of days before hatching, place a piece of sponge in the water in the pan to increase the evaporating surface area and therefore the humidity ready for hatching.

WORKING OUT THE HUMIDITY EXACTLY

This only works in a still air incubator and, should you be using one of these, it is as well to work it out. Water evaporates and, as it does, causes cooling, as every schoolchild scientist will tell you. If you measure the temperature difference between a wet and a dry thermometer, you can then work out how much water is in the air.

	Wet thermometer temperature	
Incubator temperature	28.6°C (83.5°F)	30.8°C (87.4°F)
37.7°C (100°F)	50% humidity	60% humidity

The air space within the egg is dependent on the temperature and humidity, so you can get a rough idea if all is well by comparing the shape and size of the space when candling the eggs.

Candling

The eggs should be incubated for between ten days and two weeks before trying to look inside to see what is happening. This process is called candling because it used to be done in a darkened room using a candle as a light source. Now a torch will do as well. The egg is removed from the incubator for the shortest length of time possible and held up to a bright light.

If there is no discernable structure, no shadow, no blood vessels and so on, you have an infertile or dead egg and it should be discarded. A good egg is one that shows blood vessels and a dark centre, which is the developing embryo.

Eggs with no structure after 14 days should not be returned to the incubator; you will not get it to go after this time. Don't eat it!

HATCHING

The chicks will eat all the remaining yolk and white in the egg and thus be ready to face the world. On day 21 you should hear them bashing away at the shell and one by one they will emerge. Adjust the temperature to 35°C (95°F).

Remove the shell as they hatch and spend some time watching and wondering; they never fail to move the observer, so savour this time.

Leave them in the incubator for them to dry out. They may be sticky as a consequence of too humid conditions or conversely too dry. Once they are all fluffy they are ready for the next stage of life.

MOVING CHICKS

No more than 24 hours after hatching, the chicks will need to be moved to a draught-free enclosure which has a heat source, chick feed and water. Carefully lift the chicks to their new surroundings. The box can have a sheet of newspaper in the bottom at first.

Hang a heating lamp over the chicks to provide warmth and watch the chicks. If they huddle together under the lamp it is too high and they are cold. If they run to the extremities of the enclosure the lamp is too low and they are too hot. Adjust the lamp so they move freely and comfortably. Try to use an infrared lamp – would you like to spend your first days of life under a bright light? White light lamps do have a psychological affect on the birds and, remember, chickens are 'imprinted'; what they see now marks their behaviour later in life.

The enclosure should be completely free from draughts and secure from the excessive attention of children and pets.

After a few days add some sawdust litter as described earlier and place some newspaper over the litter, especially near the food and water, to help the chicks walk about in their first week of life.

You might have to teach them to eat by picking crumbs from the food tray and dropping them near the chick. Similarly the water should be provided in a way that the chicks cannot drown.

Room temperature

Although the chicks need a lamp to keep them warm, the temperature of the room is important too. It you are able to work comfortably in shirt sleeves in the first week this is fine. Gradually, over the first few weeks the temperature can be reduced. For the best results, keep an eye on the birds, watching how they move, huddle, eat and drink.

EXPECT MORTALITY

You are not going to bring every egg to point of lay. First of all, some eggs might not be viable and you will have disposed of them in the early weeks of incubation. Secondly, the stragglers, those who do not hatch well, are frequently ill equipped for life and they can die very early in the first week of life. Thirdly, there will be some who die for unexplained reasons or as a mishap. If you have got two-thirds of your eggs through to adulthood, you have done well.

DAILY ROUTINE

Week 1

Check the temperature regularly and that the birds are moving freely. Clean receptacles and replace food and water. Change bedding where appropriate.

Make sure there are no draughts and remove any chicks that might have died. Check to see that all chicks are eating and drinking.

Maintain good lighting during the day, but not too bright. Make sure there is plenty of ventilation in the room whilst maintaining temperature.

Week 2

As for week 1 but add a little grit to the food – of an appropriate size for the chicks. Cool the room a little, but in all other aspects of care maintain the regime. Add sawdust bedding.

Weeks 3–5

Make sure the birds have more space to move around, increasingly giving them more room. Raise the lamp a little and give them the opportunity to warm up under the lamp and then cool down. Keep up with the feeding regime and watch for the temperature tolerance of the birds. Don't allow them to pant.

Weeks 6–8

Start in week 6 to add some growers pellets (or mash) to the feed, a little each day until by week 8 they are eating growers ration. Also increase the size of the grit a little. A small amount of cod liver oil dripped into the feed is a good idea for a vitamin boost – but no more than a teaspoon full.

Increase their space and then think about moving them outside.

In week 8 turn the lamp off during the day unless it is freezing cold, leaving it on during the night. This will harden up the birds and then, the following week, leave it off altogether. By now they should all be on growers ration completely. Have them on this ration for at least a week before they are moved.

Weeks 9–10

Move the birds to a separate coop and keep them indoors, especially if the weather is wet and cold. Keep your eye on them because this is a stressful time for them. Deter them from pecking each other.

Weeks 11–12 and onwards

By now, assuming the weather is good, the birds should have their own run and be beginning to live a normal hen existence. Add worming powder to the feed since they are scratching soil and eating grubs. Try to run them on virgin soil if you can, or at least soil that has had a year's worth of rest from poultry.

Introducing new hens to older ones

Take your time. It should be at least 18 to 20 weeks before the stock can be merged. Run them in close but separate pens together for a week for them to get to know each other. Make sure you have the room in the hut for the newcomers and ensure the hut is spotlessly clean and deloused.

Keep a close eye on the birds when you introduce them and be prepared to remove bullies or victims.

VACCINATION

People rarely vaccinate their new home-incubated hens, which is a shame because there are a lot of diseases out there. You should always worm them as a very basic requirement, but vaccinating them can be more difficult because the industry tends to sell serums in large doses for large flocks, and if you only have six you are in danger of using too much or simply wasting money.

Chapter 6 discussed a regime for poultry inoculation and you should consider this if you are going to keep a larger flock, if you are going to show your birds and if they are to encounter lots of wildlife.

The best way to buy inoculation products is to go along to your local supplier of hens and ask their advice because supply varies greatly. This is information you need before you start to incubate your eggs; some research into your locality will prove useful.

CHAPTER 8

THE EGG

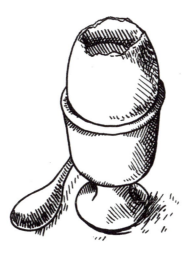

The hen's egg is the most versatile and complete food, wrapped in its own shell for protection and storage. It remains fresh because, to a certain extent, there are living cells inside it. The evolution of the egg has provided reptiles and birds with a successful way of producing offspring, though it is not perfect. An egg can become cold thus killing the occupant, it does not allow the proper growth of membranes unless it is almost constantly moved around, and its membranes allow only a small amount of gaseous exchange and consequently its occupants could never grow to a decent size. The ostrich egg is the limit of this evolutionary technique.

The ability of the egg to stop development until a trigger occurs (usually the heat from mother's bottom) is a remarkable evolutionary strategy, allowing all the chicks to be born on the same day – there is safety in numbers, and consequently hens lay an egg a day until they have enough to form a clutch.

We use this trait when we collect eggs for use. If you have a cockerel who is successfully mating with the hens, your eggs will be fertile. But when you take them for use in the kitchen there is no tiny chick inside and you wouldn't know this was a fertilised egg. This is because the egg has been kept cool and consequently its development has yet to begin.

So, for all culinary intents fertilised and unfertilised eggs are the same so long as they have not been incubated.

THE ASSEMBLY LINE

Like all females, a hen hatches with all the eggs she will need during her life already inside her in their initial form. Biologically speaking, the answer to the question, 'What comes first, the chicken or the egg?' is easy – it's the egg!

Obviously an egg represents a significant investment for the bird in water, energy and nutrients and she will produce eggs at the expense of her own wellbeing for a while until she becomes sick. A sick hen does not lay well.

Similar to a human ovary, an egg is released into the oviduct each day. If there is a cockerel about there is likely to be sperm waiting for it, but the egg will remain at the head of the oviduct for around 30 minutes waiting for fertilisation. This explains the repeated attentions cockerels have for the hen, so that viable sperm can be in situ ready for when ovulation takes place.

THE EGG'S CONSTRUCTION

The egg is built in layers from the yolk and its membrane, then the white and its supporting structures, an outer membrane and finally the shell. The inner membrane acts as a template upon which the shell is laid in the final stages of development. This membrane is not attached at the blunt end of the egg and forms an air space, which grows as the egg ages and in particular as the chick develops.

POO ON MY EGGS

Any staining on an egg can be washed off. It is usually there because the bird has messy feet, so some bedding nearby will help dry their feet. The way the system at the vent works is that the egg completely closes off the intestine so that none of its contents can escape. However, should the nest box be heavily soiled and should there be blood in evidence you might need to check your hens to see nothing is amiss.

HOW TO COLLECT EGGS

The impulse of hens to find for themselves a little dished out shape, enclosed a little on all sides, with some bedding to act as insulation, is very strong. Provide a little hen-sized box that looks warm and inviting and she will prefer to lay in it. A hen that lays sporadically around the place, sometimes in soil, sometimes in grass and nowhere near the nest box, should be picked up and carefully placed in the nest box until she stops.

Sharing cubicles

Unless a hen is going broody, she will share a nest box with the other birds. On the whole you need one box for every five birds, but a spare one will help stop the poor hens from having to queue to lay. Broody hens fiercely defend their box.

In order to keep down the transmission of external parasites make sure the bedding is changed regularly. If you can build the bottom of your nest box with wire, some will fall through. I try to change the straw every week, giving the area a good wipe at the same time.

Always try to collect eggs at the same time. I don't like leaving eggs in a hot house in the summer and, since I only have a few eggs, the amusing 'squark' given off by my hens when they have laid is the cue for me to collect them.

I collect my eggs daily at noon, but I work from home so you might have a different regime. Take your neighbour through the way you collect your eggs just in case you need them to do it for you. If you leave eggs in the nest box you run the risk of one of your hens getting broody, or one of the more clumsy ladies breaking them. Should that happen you will find the hens rushing to eat the egg, behaviour that can lead to other things such as cannibalism, bullying and feather pecking, and that clearly should be avoided.

Access
Hens are not fussy birds but they do get a little territorial about their nesting. If you have access to the eggs from outside the hut (somewhat like a robbing fox might) without having to walk into the hut and collect the eggs, all the better.

STORING AND PRESERVING EGGS
A pile of eggs is a great thrill in the kitchen. But it is best not to store them for long periods – give them away to your neighbours, family and friends. In an urban situation you are unlikely to have a glut of eggs since you will have only a few hens, but on an allotment it's a different matter and you might have a lot more. Eggs will store for 21 days in the air. You can keep them in the fridge, but allow them to warm up before use. This will add another week to their life.

How to freeze an egg
Always freeze the freshest eggs you have. Don't have a glut and then decide to freeze the old ones; cook the old ones and freeze the new.

They don't freeze too well in their shell and you have to be careful with the yolks. The easiest freezing method is to break the egg and lightly whisk the whites and yolks together as for an omelette. Then fill an ice cube tray with the mixture and freeze it. Two egg cubes equal one large egg. Defrost slowly overnight ready for use the next day.

Freezing whole eggs is more difficult. You have to break the yolk a bit to stop it from going lumpy when it freezes. This makes them useless for the perfect fried egg!

If you want to freeze yolks alone, add the tip of a teaspoon of salt to every four egg yolks. This stops them becoming lumpy or gelled.

Other ways of preserving eggs

One of the reasons why eggs go off is that the shell is porous and the contents are not sterile. However you can slow their decay by blocking the holes in the shell. This is done by immersing the egg in water glass, which is sodium silicate solution. The holes in the shell are blocked and the egg lasts for around four months as long as it remains in the solution. The container must be air tight and kept in a cool place. When removed, the egg will keep for around another month. This method has been used for hundreds of years and the eggs are not damaged or tainted in any way because of the process.

Pickled eggs

Pickling uses vinegar and a little spice to preserve the egg once it has been cooked. This makes the egg into a boiled salad treat, although not much use for cooking. You will need:

A dozen free range, very fresh eggs

1.2 l white vinegar

25 g readymade pickling spice

8 whole cloves

1. Hard boil the eggs and leave to cool completely in very cold water.

2. Pour the vinegar into a pan with the spices in a muslin bag. Bring to the boil and simmer for 10 minutes. Leave to cool before removing the spice bag.

3. Pour some of the cooled vinegar into a sterilised jar, to about a quarter of the way up the jar. Sterilise the jar by either boiling, heating in the oven or by using sterilising tablets.

4. Remove the egg shells and put the eggs into the jar. Fill the jar with the vinegar and seal it immediately.

The eggs will be ready to eat in 5 to 6 weeks.

COOKING EGGS

In a way writing this section is an impossible task. A huge number of dishes and sauces have eggs as their foundation, so this could be one of the longest chapters in the world. But I do have a bee in my bonnet about the frying of eggs, for which I will give detailed instructions later. (Well, they *have* to be perfect!)

Eating eggs is good for you

In recent years there has been talk about cholesterol and eggs. It has been widely reported that if you eat a lot of eggs you will get a subsequent boost of the wrong type of cholesterol. Actual research has shown this to be completely untrue. Studies of body builders (who regularly eat 18 eggs a day) comparing them to ordinary members of the public have shown there to be no difference between high and low consumption when it comes to cholesterol levels.

There is a body of research that shows eating eggs can actually lower cholesterol levels because they're high in cholesterol but low in saturated fats. In other words, the body regulates the amount of cholesterol in the blood and if you eat eggs the body stops producing its own.

The good news is that you are no more in danger of a heart attack from eating eggs than anyone else on an average diet.

Raw eggs

If you are going to use your eggs raw in any food you really need to ensure the appropriate vaccinations have been administered – particularly for salmonella. If you have bought hens from a good dealer you should be able to ask about their vaccination status. If you buy ex-battery hens you can be guaranteed they have been vaccinated to the limit of what the law allows.

How to fry an egg

Why is this here? Because this book is on a mission to bring back the perfect fried egg! For a start you need an egg that had just been laid. (That is why I collect my eggs at noon, and now you can guess what is my favourite lunch!)

The pan should be hot but not too hot. On a scale of 1 to 6 on my electric hob, I choose 5 to start, so it's not quite full heat. The pan should have a tablespoon of oil and a knob of butter. In cooking the rule is oil for frying, butter for flavour. Let the fat come to heat and then crack the egg with a very sharp knife. Don't bash it on the side of the pan, and only make a small crack, enough to get your thumbs on either side to pull outwards, thus opening the egg.

Get your hands around the egg above the hot pan and open it, carefully spilling the contents from no higher than an inch or two above the hot surface. Then, once the egg is in the pan, turn the heat down to half (3 in my case).

You should see the golden yolk sitting pert and proud of the white, which should solidify fairly quickly, not running about the pan in a wasteful manner.

When all the white is solid, use a spoon to baste the yolk two or three times, thus cooking the top membrane, but leaving the gorgeous yolk runny and full of flavour!

CHAPTER 9

GETTING HELP

When you take on poultry, wherever you are, you will find yourself part of a community going back thousands of years. In the early days of the British Isles Bronze Age peoples had the joy of keeping (and eating) chickens. They were traded all over the world, and whereas these shores represented the very ends of civilisation, we had rich supplies of ores that drove the Pre Ancient world – copper and tin in particular. Consequently traders from afar would bring not only precious metals such as gold, but oil, grain and poultry. The feeling of warmth when collecting eggs was shared by peoples before you for many hundreds of generations. Poultry link their owners with the distant past.

This community is strongly represented in modern days by a huge number of poultry keepers, many of them associated with one group or another, some of which we shall look at below. Still more are loners who have no affiliations but are nevertheless a rich resource for help. Seek out people to share your experiences and follow, or at least think about, their advice.

BIO-SECURITY

Commercial battery or shed poultry companies spend a fortune on bio-security. They ensure their birds live in almost hermetically clean conditions and that nothing enters or leaves the shed without control. The ordinary poultry keeper cannot hope for such a system, and probably wouldn't want one.

However, The Poultry Club of Great Britain has produced an etiquette regarding bio-security, which means stopping cross contamination to your birds (or anyone else's) and is basically common sense. This should become the norm when you are meeting any person and their poultry. I have added a bit to it too, regarding footwear and sharing equipment.

- Keep feed in a way that it does not attract wild birds

- Supply clean water every day

- Have an effective way of controlling vermin

- Keep new birds separate for three weeks

- Birds taken to a show should be quarantined for a week

- Wear cleanable boots and overalls when dealing with your poultry

- Change overalls and disinfect boots before and after visiting other poultry keepers or sales

- Disinfect boots before dealing with your poultry

- Do not share equipment

- Wash hands before and after handling poultry

If you are given any equipment or wish to give any away, always disinfect it. You don't need anything stronger than Milton solution or the various preparations designed for cleaning wine bottles, but always wear rubber gloves. If you have anything soiled with chicken poo you need to use hot soapy water to remove it, and then disinfect afterwards.

GETTING HELP WITH ILLNESS AND FINDING A POULTRY VET

This section could have supplied a list of vets, but the information would become less useful as details changed. As the internet is flexible enough to keep pace with changes, we prefer to direct you to online information.

Elsewhere I have hinted that finding a vet that is good with poultry is no mean task, and once you find someone you will be advised to keep him or her close. There are a number of websites that can give you more information and point you in the right direction. Also your feed supplier will be able to help you with the major things you need, wormers, insect and mite treatments, and so on.

A company who deal in Cotswold Legbar hens have a very helpful website from which you will be able to find a poultry vet near you: www. legbarsofbroadway.co.uk They screen the vets to see if they have either a poultry specialist or a poultry department. So far they have vets' details in the following counties: Cambridgeshire, Derbyshire, Devon, East Sussex, Glouces-tershire, Herefordshire, Kent, Norfolk, Northamptonshire, Northumberland, Nottinghamshire, Shropshire, Somerset, Wales, Warwickshire, West Sussex and Yorkshire. The list is growing.

The Omlet Forum has a section on finding a poultry vet, which is also useful. It is a good idea to post a question on this forum too – if you need a vet in a certain area, for example, someone is most likely to respond to you. Go to http://club.omlet.co.uk/forum and search 'poultry vets'. Omlet is a company specialising in the production of plastic housing and has an active support base of over 20,000 users. There should be someone who knows a poultry vet in your area, or has experienced the same problems as you.

POULTRY CLUBS

An excellent source of help, encouragement, feed, materials and equipment are the various poultry clubs dotted around the country. There is usually at least one such club in every large town and certainly in every county.

The Poultry Club of Great Britain

This is the club for people interested in pure breeds or who want to show their birds. They have a lot of information for all poultry keepers on their website and you can become a member. Founded in 1877, they are interested in all pure and traditional breeds of poultry, both in Great Britain and throughout the world. They have controlled the specifications of all pure breed poultry over the years and provide a book, *British Poultry Standards*.

After 1848, when cockfighting was outlawed in the UK, the poultry keepers that used to meet for this purpose decided to meet together in competitions to see not which bird was the best fighter, but which conformed more closely to a specific standard. This is fundamentally the raison d'être of The Poultry Club.

The club also has standards for eggs that are shown at various shows. If you wish to get into breeding pure strains of poultry, especially for showing, The Poultry Club of Great Britain is an important starting point. You will get much out of the membership and there are shows to attend all over the country.

CONTACTING THE POULTRY CLUB OF GREAT BRITAIN
They can be found at most agricultural shows around the country and also at their website: www.poultryclub.org. You can email them on info@poultryclub.org. Their president is a lovely chap with the splendid name of Mr Hatcher. You can write to The Poultry Club, Keeper's Cottage, 40 Benvarden Road, Dervock, Ballymoney, Country Antrim BT53 6NN.

The Rare Poultry Society

This society was started in 1969 to include the numerous breeds that were once strong in the UK, but had for the most part fallen into decline. They are somewhat like The Poultry Club of Great Britain but in some cases are interested in birds where there might be as few as one breeder. They are also interested in breeds that have not yet become established in the UK. Like The Poultry Club, they have shows and information on the breeds they are interested in. You can find their range of breeds on their website: www.rarepoultrysociety.co.uk but they have plans to increase the range of birds they cover, and produce a breed book of their own. Membership brings with it a newsletter and breeders' contacts. They hope in the future to publish their own set of breed specifications.

Utility Poultry Breeders Association

This group is interested in using pure breed hens because they have a considerable inbuilt disease resistance, but they wish to increase their productivity, especially egg laying. They have found that in the United Kingdom poultry breeds have lost many of their large breeders, so that the genetic strains of a lot of important breeds are seriously in danger of being lost. The Utility Breeders Association is determined to replace and improve these genetic strains.

They can be found online at www.utilitypoultry.co.uk and they are on the lookout for people who have rare breed hens that seem to be laying well.

Pure Breed Clubs

The following details are for the breeds mentioned in this book which I have decided, for better or worse, are best for urban poultry keeping.

Ancona Club

Mr Phil Smedley
Email: phil.boy@virgin.net
Tel: 01904 468387

Australorp Club

Email: ian@australorpclubgb.wanadoo.co.uk
Tel: 01636 814958
There is a website: www.poultryclub.org/australorpclubgb/index.htm which is a bit of a mouthful, but you'll get there in the end.

The British Barnevelder Club

Mr G Broadhurst
Tel: 01630 638630
This has always been a strong club.

Black Rock

There is no club really but the main breeder (only for some years) is Mr Peter Siddons.
Email: a500sho@googlemail.co.uk
Tel: 01968 677014

Brahma – there are a number of contacts for Brahmas:

The Brahma Club

Mrs Sue Black
Tel: 01792 898310

The International Brahma Club
Mr David Osborne
12 Tintern House, Selcroft Avenue
Harborne
Birmingham B32 2BS
England
Email: TIBC@cresum.demon.co.uk
Website: www.feathersite.com/Poultry/CGA/Brahma/BRKBrahma.html

Buff Orpington Club
Mr P. Smedley
Tel: 01904 468387
There is an interesting website at www.orpy.demon.co.uk/The%20Orpington%20Breed%20of%20Fowl.htm

Leghorn Club
A great club and super website with loads of information.
Mr Richard Grice
Tel: 01833 660260
Website: www.theleghornclub.com

Marans Club
Mr A Heeks
Tel: 01270 882189

www.marans.co.uk is a great website though it has nothing to do with the Marans Club.

Marsh Daisy
Rare Poultry Society
Mr Richard Billso
Alexandra Cottage, 8 St Thomas's Road

Great Glen
Leicestershire LE8 OEG
England

The New Hampshire Red Club (Great Britain)
Mrs C Compton
Devonia, Weston Lane
Micheldever, Winchester
Hampshire SO21 3AH
England
Tel: 01962 774476

The Plymouth Rock Club
Email: information@theplymouthrockclub.co.uk
There is a great website at http://theplymouthrockclub.co.uk/
There are lots of groups around the country and this is an excellent club to join.

Rhode Island Red
There is a good website at www.feathersite.com/Poultry/CGP/Reds/BRKRIR.html

The Rhode Island Red Club
Mr Richard Everett
Crossways, Kerries Road
South Brent
Devon TQ10 9DE
England
Tel: 01364 73294

The Scottish Rhode Island Red Club
Mr David Bruce
24 Biggar Rd

Libberton, Carnwath
Strathclyde ML11 8LX
Scotland
Tel: 01555 840867

www.crohio.com/reds/ is a great website but it is an American site.
Sussex Club
Miss S Raisey
Tel: 01823 672789

HELP WITH HYBRID HENS

By their nature, hybrids are the simple red/brown commercial hens which are produced in their millions, probably born in a huge hatching machine. Whereas they are loved by their owners, there are no groups or clubs you can go to for help. The reality of the matter, biologically speaking, is they are just as pure bred as the other so called pure breeds because all hens are hybrids of one form or another. All hens were 'developed' at some time or another and maybe we will be talking of pure breed Mrs Pepperpot hens in a hundred years time – and isn't it a shame people don't breed this bird anymore?

The breed societies will not leave you helpless, particularly The Poultry Club of Great Britain. Although they do not have a remit for hybrid birds, they do have members in all areas of the UK.

There are a number of other sources of help:

Battery Hen Welfare Trust

The Battery Hen Welfare Trust was set up in order to bring battery hens to people who both want them and can keep them compassionately. They have no axe to grind with the poultry industry and recognise they are solely there to re-house hens rather than see them killed at the beginning of their first moult.

There are a number of coordinators and helpers around the country and they are completely expert in the raising and care of hybrid hens.

There is an excellent website: www.bhwt.org.uk/ that will give you a local contact near you. There is also a care line, which you can call and ask any question you like from an expert on the end of the phone who has the appropriate information. They are particularly good at answering feeding problems because they are sponsored by a feed company. However they will help you as much as possible on all problems.

You can call the care line on 01362 822904 or email bhwtcareline@ smallholderfeed.co.uk

Omlet

This is a commercial company producing the very popular Eglu chicken house as well as a range of hybrid hens. A large number of the owners of these houses keep hybrid hens. There are 20,000 owners and most of these people are internet users. The Omlet forum at is a good place to register for help and support, even if you do not have one of their products. The forum is full of people keeping chickens and they have the same experiences as everyone else. Post a question and you are guaranteed a number of responses. You can find the Omlet Forum at http://club.omlet.co.uk/forum/

They also arrange 'Hen Parties', which are an introduction to keeping poultry at either the beginner or advanced level, and there are hundreds of them around the country.

PUBLICATIONS

There are a number of magazines that deal with poultry. The more general ones include *Country Smallholding*, *Home Farmer* and *Smallholder*. These include poultry articles alongside other articles on gardening and keeping livestock. *Practical Poultry* magazine is specifically written for poultry keepers. *Fancy Fowl* is for people who are looking to show their birds and it has a listing of prize winners as well as interesting articles on poultry keeping.

GLOSSARY

Air sack	Large spaces in the bird which inflate and deflate, forcing air over the tissues of the lung.
Albumen	The white portion of the egg.
Arc	A wooden A-frame hen house for a few hens.
Bantam	A miniature chicken often identical to the larger breed. Although small, they often prefer to roam and are not that suitable for small urban spaces.
Bedding	Material laid on the floor of the hut for comfort, insulation and soaking up faeces.
Broiler	A chicken bred for the kitchen, often in large industrial-type sheds. They are usually killed at 18 weeks of age.
Broodiness	A chicken that is preparing to sit on eggs in order to hatch them.

Candle	A method for seeing inside an egg to check if it is fertile and developing into a chick.
Carnivorous	Any animal that eats meat alone as the majority of its diet.
Chalzae	The protein strands in an egg that act to keep the yolk central in the egg.
Clipped wing	Cutting through the flight feathers of a single wing to stop the bird from flying.
Cloaca	Meaning 'sewer', it is the final opening of the digestive system, also known as the vent.
Coccidia/Coccidiosis	Bacteria found in the environment that causes illness in birds and mammals.
Cock/Cockerel	A cock is older than 12 months. The cockerel is younger than 12 months.
Comb	The red membrane on the chicken's head. It indicates fertility and cools the bird, and it is often a target for attack.
Crop	The first sack of the digestive system which contains grit to grind food.
Cross-linked sexing	Also known as auto sexing. Crossing a male of one breed with a female of another frequently produces offspring in which the males have different plumage and so are easily spotted at hatching.
Cull	To kill ill birds or to reduce the numbers of unwanted birds.
Dislocation	The only method allowed for killing birds without first stunning.

Egg tooth	The beak of the chick is designed to crack the egg and is frequently referred to as the egg tooth.
Eglu	A plastic hen hut of modern design.
Feeder/Hopper	The many kinds of receptacles for feeding hens. In an urban garden it is best to have a single dish that is replenished, but further afield a hopper system is fine.
Grit	Birds need a supply of grit for grinding food in the crop.
Hackle	The feathered area as the breast meets the neck.
Herbivore	Any animal that eats only plant matter for the majority of its diet.
Hut	A house for chickens that can take various forms. For example, Arc is an A-frame based hut and Eglu is a plastic design. There are a large number of designs available, from converted garden sheds to small huts. Wire-based runs are frequently attached.
Hybrid	A bird whose parentage comes from two distinctly different breeds.
Incubator	A mechanical and electrical machine for hatching eggs.
Leptospirosis	Bacterial infection passed on from rat's urine.
Mareks	A viral infection of poultry that can cause tumours.
Mash	Pre-prepared food for chickens which is similar to pellets but in milled form.
Moult	Birds replace their feathers once a year, under hormonal control. It coincides with the changing of egg laying in females.

Nest box	A quiet secluded box for hens to lay in.
Omnivore	Any animal that eats animal and vegetable matter.
Panting	Birds do not sweat and therefore control their temperature by choosing shade, drinking water and panting.
Pecking order	Hens arrange themselves with a certain amount of dominance. You need to be careful that the dominant hens are not causing damage or bullying too much, especially when it comes to access to feed.
Pellets	Food for hens in pelleted form, usually a complete diet ration.
Perch	A rod or bar on which hens sleep above the ground as though in a tree.
Plumage	The bird's complete coat of feathers.
Point of Lay (POL)	Point of lay is when a bird will start to lay and can occur anywhere between 18 and 24 weeks.
Predator	Any animal that might kill and eat your poultry.
Proventriculus	The first part of the stomach, often used to refer to the whole stomach.
Pure breed	Hens that hatch male and female chicks which share common characteristics and always breed true.
Ration	A feeding regime designed for perfect development of chicks, constant laying of eggs, growing meat and maintaining the birds' health.
Red mite	Mites that spend the day time in the hut and the night time on the birds sucking their blood.

Run	A covered and fenced area for chickens to move around, usually outside.
Saddle	The back area around the shoulders.
Scales	The legs are covered with overlapping plates of skin, which can become infected.
Scaly legs	Infection of the leg often caused by infestation.
Vaccination	A series of drugs available to prevent chicks getting or passing on various diseases.
Vent/Cloaca	The bottom at the bottom of the bird. There is no vaginal opening in birds. The eggs are laid through the same opening, but a mechanism separates both important processes.
Vitelline	This refers to the yolk, and the vitelline membrane is the demarcation between the yolk and the white.
Waterer	Usually an upturned bucket that fits into a special 'lid' that acts as a dish when the whole thing is upturned.
Wattle	Flesh hanging from the face by the beak, often red like the comb.
Wing bar	Brighter feathers on the wing that cover the flight feathers.

INDEX